Who Is This **Monster (or Treasure)** in My House?

Who Is This Monster (or Treasure) In My House?
Copyright © 2021 by Kate Mason.
All rights reserved.

Published by Grammar Factory Publishing, an imprint of MacMillan Company Limited.

No part of this book may be used or reproduced in any manner whatsoever without the prior written permission of the author, except in the case of brief passages quoted in a book review or article. All enquiries should be made to the author.

Grammar Factory Publishing
MacMillan Company Limited
25 Telegram Mews, 39th Floor, Suite 3906
Toronto, Ontario, Canada
M5V 3Z1

www.grammarfactory.com

Mason, Kate-
Who is This Monster (or Treasure) in My House? / Kate Mason.

Paperback ISBN 978-1-989737-34-7
eBook ISBN 978-1-989737-35-4

    1. FAM034000 FAMILY & Relationships / Parenting / General 2. PSY023000 PSYCHOLOGY / Personality. 3. FAM046000 FAMILY & RELATIONSHIPS / Life Stages / General.

Production Credits
Printed in Australia by IngramSpark
Cover design by Designerbility
Interior layout design by Dania Zafar
Book production and editorial services by Grammar Factory Publishing

Grammar Factory's Carbon Neutral Publishing Commitment
From January 1st, 2020 onwards, Grammar Factory Publishing is proud to be neutralizing the carbon footprint of all printed copies of its authors' books printed by or ordered directly through Grammar Factory or its affiliated companies through the purchase of Gold Standard-Certified International Offsets.

The Myers-Briggs Type Indicator® and MBTI® are registered trademarks of the Myers-Briggs Type Indicator Trust in the USA and other countries.

Disclaimer
The material in this publication is of the nature of general comment only and does not represent professional advice. It is not intended to provide specific guidance for particular circumstances, and it should not be relied on as the basis for any decision to take action or not take action on any matter which it covers. Readers should obtain professional advice where appropriate, before making any such decision. To the maximum extent permitted by law, the author and publisher disclaim all responsibility and liability to any person, arising directly or indirectly from any person taking or not taking action based on the information in this publication.

Who Is This **Monster (or Treasure)** in My House?

A PARENT'S GUIDE TO UNDERSTANDING PERSONALITY
TYPES TO BETTER CONNECT WITH YOUR KIDS

Kate Mason

ABOUT THE AUTHOR

Kate Mason is passionate about people, personalities and parenting. Bringing these three things together is what creates harmonious and happy relationships in business and at home.

As a qualified personality coach, international keynote speaker, business owner and school teacher, her mission is to help others understand the innate personalities of those around them so that they can build stronger, richer, more successful lives.

Kate has spent the last forty years using personality tools such as the Myers-Briggs Type Indicator on her family, on her friends, and in business. She has witnessed the enormous changes that can be made in human dynamics when we learn to understand our monsters and work out where to find the treasures in our relationships.

Building the skills required to value each other's strengths and limitations, and having open conversations in which each person's view is heard and valued, is crucial. Helping our offspring accept when they are wrong, developing their self-worth, teaching them the difference between bullying and constructive criticism, and making them feel loved and safe enough to express their own opinions is a parental dream that Kate believes is possible!

She believes that educating parents about their family's personalities will ultimately bring into the world something that is missing today: a strong, resilient and emotionally intelligent generation.

As a partner and mother of two, Kate uses facts, fun and humour to help you communicate successfully with everyone in your life.

As this book will show.

thepersonalitycoach.com.au

ACKNOWLEDGEMENTS

Just as this book was about to go to print I found myself stuck in hotel quarantine, thanks to COVID-19, with my husband and two children. Being trapped in a tiny room and unable to leave, even with the people you love the most, can bring out the worst in all of us. Talk about intense!

That is why I am forever grateful for my knowledge and understanding of personalities, particularly my husband's, as I could quite easily have 'killed' him many times while we were stuck in that hotel room together. As we closed our businesses for the second time, my Introverted Thinking husband drove me crazy as he dwelled on every possible disaster that might happen. As an Extraverted Feeling Type, I insisted on seeing the glass half full, and desperately missed the external world full of people. I began to feel and act like a caged animal.

Fortunately, we know and understand ourselves and each other, and were able to talk through and acknowledge our fears and stresses. We could plan how to actually enjoy our time together – even in lockdown! Had we not had the skills to work things out, we would have been in constant disagreement and full of anger.

I am so grateful to be able to share with you what I have learned over the last forty years so that you can navigate any potential disasters in your relationships – just as I did while in that hotel room!

But that would not have been possible without critical, key people behind me.

So, to Paul, Jack and Cassie, my long-suffering family, for their love and encouragement on this lifelong journey of personality discovery – thank you. And thank you for allowing me to showcase your Types to the world.

To Lora, who has been with me every step of the way as I 'gave birth' to my book baby. Without her dedication, superb structuring skills and never-ending belief in me and my story, I would never have made it.

To Celeste, who has spent many hours helping me find my voice in my writing.

To my friends and family, who read and critiqued my book and helped me keep moving forward.

To the following people: Heather, Paul, Sally, Millie, and Lora, who have allowed me to use their wonderful stories to demonstrate the power of understanding who you are and who you live with.

And to you, the reader. I am so excited for the journey of discovery you're about to embark on. I know it will change your life like it has changed mine.

CONTENTS

Introduction   1

PART 1:
Finding the 'diamonds' in yourself and your partner   **11**

    Chapter 1: Extravert or Introvert Parent/Partner   15
    Chapter 2: Sensing or Intuitive Parent/Partner   25
    Chapter 3: Thinking or Feeling Parent/Partner   35
    Chapter 4: Judging or Perceiving Parent/Partner   45

Part 1: Action: Summarise your Personality Type   **55**

PART 2:
Finding the personality 'jewels' in your child/children   **57**

    Chapter 5: Extravert or Introvert Child   61
    Chapter 6: Sensing or Intuitive Child   71
    Chapter 7: Thinking or Feeling Child   79
    Chapter 8: Judging or Perceiving Child   89

Part 2: Action: Summarise your child's Personality Type   **97**

PART 3:
Finding the 'gold' in your relationships with your child/children   **99**

    Chapter 9: Extravert – Introvert Parent/Child Relationships   101
    Chapter 10: Sensing – Intuition Parent/Child Relationships   119
    Chapter 11: Thinking – Feeling Parent/Child Relationships   139
    Chapter 12: Judging – Perceiving Parent/Child Relationships   161

    Conclusion   179
    Resources   186
    Appendix: Active listening   187

INTRODUCTION

Have you ever had a day like this...

The school morning has started. You're running late; not unusual, but stressful for all concerned.

The nagging begins; not from you, but from everyone else. Your son is stressed, and his morning routine is messed up by your insistence that he hurry – he doesn't have time to complete his regular tasks to his usual standard. Your daughter is busy organising her personal life, rather than packing her lunch and schoolbag and brushing her teeth. She pesters you with questions, asking you and your husband if she can have four of her favourite friends over after school. You want to agree, but your husband can't understand her need to see more people just after she had friends over on the weekend. He mentions that he worries about your son's apparent lack of friends, and would rather see some of *them* around the place. Annoyed, he shouts at your daughter that he wants to have just one night of peace and quiet!

You bundle your disgruntled tribe into the car, while your frustrated husband drives off in a huff. Getting into the car, both kids are complaining – for different reasons. Your son is embarrassed because you never get him to school on time and your daughter is angry because her social life has not been organised. You drop them at school and drive away, breathing a huge sigh of relief that you'll have at least seven hours of peace while they're at school.

Then after school, it all starts up again. Your kids grunt hello as they climb in the car, and the rest of the journey home is spent in silence as they fiddle with their phones, ear buds firmly in place and music blaring. At home, you ask about their day. If you're lucky, they answer. Then they disappear into their bedrooms.

You visualise the years ahead and worry that the lack of communication between you all is preventing you from building loving, long-term family relationships.

You're left wondering, 'Who are these kids I'm living with? Am I ever going to be able to communicate with them?'

Does this sound all too familiar?

I bet it does! And that's why you're here…

WHY CAN'T I GET THIS RIGHT?

Parents – this is not what we signed up for! We were not told that we might end up not understanding, or even liking, our little treasures. No-one writes about that in 'expert' parenting books. And family breakdowns are becoming more common in our time-poor world, where often our personal relationships are put on the back burner while we try desperately to keep up with our busy lifestyles.

We need to have homes and relationships that our children can come to for comfort, unconditional love and advice – even when they don't really think they need it. Creating a safe, harmonious home and family life enables your children to handle the inevitable challenges of growing up in the modern world. Those challenges include being bullied, experiencing the unkindness of others, and navigating the ever-changing, potentially dangerous world of social media. Your children need to understand how to build positive friendships and be resilient enough to resist social pressures. They have to be prepared to deal with mental health issues, and the issues around sex, alcohol and drugs that are insidiously pervading our children's lives earlier and earlier.

However, if you're having trouble and your family sounds like the one

INTRODUCTION

in the story above, that does NOT make you a bad parent. If you can love your child and they feel loved, they can survive most things.

So, what's actually going on here? Why are so many parents struggling?

We only know and understand our own unique views of the world, not our children's! You are a good parent, but will become an even BETTER parent when you have the right tools to parent the treasures that your unique child has to offer.

Our problems lie in the fact that we have not been given a roadmap for parenting offspring who might be very different from us.

Wouldn't it be absolute gold if you could understand what makes your kids tick and communicate with them in their own language? Imagine the joy of getting along really well with the people you love – with no fights in the car! This is possible, but to achieve this dream it is imperative that you find out more about your child's innate needs and communication style so that you can meet them where they are – instead of trying to get them to meet you at your level.

Relationships can be hard work and there is no manual for child rearing. But discovering yours, your partner's and your child's inborn personality will help you manage those monster moments when you cannot understand how they see the world and why you are unable to communicate with them successfully.

Once you work out your child's individual personality and can see the world through their eyes, you have the knowledge and insight to be able to parent them like never before.

TIME TO TALK ABOUT PERSONALITY TYPE

So, what do we mean by our personality, and more specifically our Personality *Type*?

The personality tool I am going to introduce you to in this book was created by a mother and daughter team – Katharine Briggs and Isabel Myers. They admired the work of the famous Swiss psychologist Carl Jung, who created many of the best-known psychological concepts and theories that are used throughout the world today. Myers and Briggs embraced Jung's theory of Psychological Type and, with his permission, intertwined their own research and learnings to create a psychological instrument called the Myers-Briggs Type Indicator (MBTI).

The MBTI was first published in 1962. Its success was worldwide, and it remains one of the most popular personality tools used in business organisations today. It is a remarkable relationship tool that has been shown to significantly improve organisational performance and team work – which is exactly why I believe it should also be used in families!

So much happens at home, in our little 'team', that it would be a mistake not to use this tool in our family relationships – they are the most important ones we have.

Just like the workplace, there are many factors that affect the overall configuration of a family's dynamic. When your family life is fractured and unhappy, it is reflected in all the decisions and daily routines that you have, so obviously we want that dynamic to be a happy and harmonious one.

Understanding Type can take a bit of practise but is well worth the effort, as you shall soon see.

HOW THE MBTI WORKS

The Myers-Briggs Type Indicator (which I shall refer to as the MBTI) is divided into four sets of preferences: **Energy**, **Information**, **Decisions** and **Lifestyle**.

These preferences look at how we view life, make decisions, and interact with and structure our outer world.

Let's quickly look at each preference.

INTRODUCTION

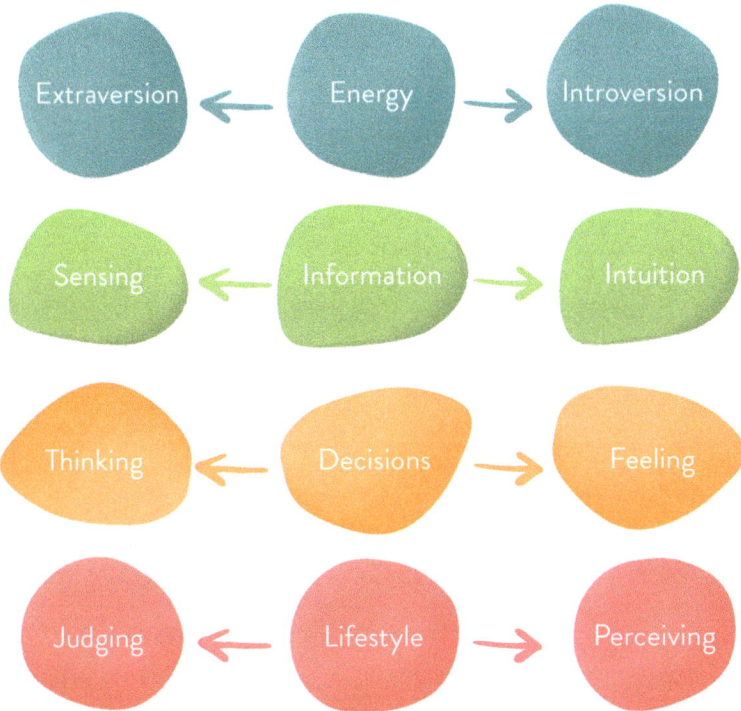

The Four Dimensions of the MBTI

1. Energy: Extraversion or Introversion?

These preferences relate to where you get your **energy** from:

EXTRAVERTS (E) get their energy from the external world of people and activities, and need regular interaction.

INTROVERTS (I) get their energy from the internal world of ideas, feelings and thoughts, and need regular downtime.

2. Information: Sensing or Intuition?

These preferences relate to the way that people take in **information**:

Sensing (S) people make sense of the world and gather information through their five senses. They enjoy details, repetition and tradition. They prefer concrete, factual information and use it to build an understanding of the bigger picture.

Intuitive (N) people gather information as patterns and connections rather than focusing on individual facts. They prefer to use their imagination, follow hunches and innovate, and enjoy abstract concepts and theories. They need to see the big picture in order to understand the parts.

3. Decisions: Thinking or Feeling?

These preferences relate to the way that people form **decisions**:

Thinking (T) Thinking Types seek *logical* reasons for making decisions. They are usually firm and fair, seek honesty and look at consequences. They ask 'Why?'

Feeling (F) Feeling Types use their *values* to make decisions. They pursue harmonious relationships, consider the impact of their decisions on other people and like to be appreciated. They ask 'Who?'

4. Lifestyle: Judging or Perceiving?

These preferences relate to how people live their **outer life** (their lifestyle):

Judging (J) Judging Types prefer an outer life that has structure and order, and they seek closure. They would agree with the motto: 'Just Do It' ... according to a fixed plan.

Perceiving (P) Perceiving Types prefer an outer life that is more flexible and enjoy exploring options that give them room for spontaneity, just in case something else comes up. They would agree with the statement: 'Let's wait and see.'

INTRODUCTION

Once you have selected one preference from each pair of preferences, you will have formed a Personality Type profile.

For example, when I choose my preferences from each of the pairs above, I am **ESFP: Extraverted, Sensing, Feeling and Perceiving.**

I prefer the outer world of people and use my senses to gather information. I use Feeling logic to make my decisions, and I enjoy mulling over many choices without having to make decisions until the last minute. I can use all of the other preferences – INTJ – but ESFP are the ones that feel like warm pyjamas and a cup of hot chocolate on a winter night.

At first, these letters might sound like gobbledygook to you (as they did to me a long time ago), but once you get to grips with them, which I will help you do over the coming pages, the results can be life changing.

I became a certified MBTI practitioner over twenty-five years ago. Being a certified practitioner – and a parent – is what qualifies me to guide you on the journey we are about to embark on together. However, I will not be using the official MBTI form in this book. Rather, my purpose is to introduce you to it in a simplified version so that you can begin your Type journey. I will help you to start looking at your precious family in a new way, begin to work them out – and have some fun at the same time! If you would like to investigate further, you can contact me or other MBTI practitioners, who can provide you with the necessary information to follow this through. Details can be found at the back of the book.

NOW OVER TO YOU...

Before you start reading, make yourself comfortable and do whatever it takes to help you find your most relaxed state of mind. As you go through the book, the information presented will help you decide what your preferences are so that you can build your own Personality Type and that of your partner and children. You will find lists of options to choose from. I want you to think about which one of the options you have the strongest preference for. When you're reading, go with the flow and try not to overthink the information. What feels the most natural to you? A lot of us feel like we're borderline in a preference, and that's okay. Or you may choose one preference, but decide to change your mind after reading further. This is okay, too. It is not a process that leads to a right or wrong answer. It is a discovery that will broaden your outlook and understanding of the people in your family and your life.

I have included space for you to record your family's Personality Types as you discover them. There are also spaces where you can record any 'aha' moments you have while reading, or learnings about the 'gold' that you discover in your family. Please also take the time to write down any observations you make at the end of the chapters. You can then refer to them when you need to, and use them to help you start putting some of your learnings into practice in your own family.

As you go through the book, hold on to the fact that we are not right or wrong – just different! And above all else, remember to have fun with this. Though it's a serious tool, it's not supposed to be so serious that you get stuck or overcomplicate it.

Just one golden nugget of insight can make a huge difference to your relationships.

Throughout the book you'll also find many stories about my life, my friends, and especially my family. I am sharing these because I love the gifts that knowing and understanding my children's and my partner's Type has given me, and I want to share them with you. I use my knowledge of Type every single day in my parenting, even now that my children are adults. Knowing this helps me manage my expectations, shows them I understand who they are, and allows me to communicate my love for them in ways that they recognise.

The key to keeping your relationships fresh and strong, and your family alive and present, lies in the next pages. I have enjoyed every minute (well, nearly every minute!) of my parenting journey so far, and I hope

INTRODUCTION

that you find lots of jewels that will create even more happiness on yours.

So, let's get to know everyone in your family, so that you're equipped with lifelong tools to help you communicate successfully with the people you love.

Kate

x

PART 1:

FINDING THE 'DIAMONDS' IN YOURSELF AND YOUR PARTNER

When I first met my husband, Paul, we fell madly, deeply in love, as you do. I was initially charmed by Paul's business-driven mind and his ability to delegate and make things happen. He was practical and helped me to see things more clearly. Paul was attracted to my easy-going, expansive outlook on life. It helped him socialise with greater ease and took the pressure off him when he was with groups of people. He also thought that I was funny, which really sealed the deal.

Paul and I were contrasting personalities. I was a 'people person', and loved being with people as much as possible, both at work and at home. Paul only reluctantly participated in the many social outings I organised, although he usually admitted to having a great time once he was there. He didn't need people around him – his main focus was his work where he enjoyed making changes and working on improvements. Paul's drive and need to push forward with decisions was important to his happiness. And it made life exciting for me – no two days were ever the same.

At first, we regarded our differences as treasures. But, as the years rolled on, we began to clash over many things, and spent much of our time caught up in anger and arguments. We didn't understand our differences, and my need for friends and good times clashed with his continual search for improvement and change. I would organise a busy social weekend, and make plans to go out on both Friday and Saturday night. This would be too much for Paul, who would pick a fight on Saturday afternoon so that I'd have to cancel our plans for the evening. On the other hand, Paul would organise business meetings and give me jobs to do, which I resented. So I would be late to the meetings, or not turn up at all, and not do the jobs he allocated to me. Because we didn't understand each other's needs, we each thought the other one was making unreasonable demands. Our treasures became our monsters, dominating and destroying our relationship.

After six years together, Paul and I found ourselves staring at each other with nothing to say but hurtful words. Neither of us could see anything we really liked about the other person anymore. We were too busy telling each other what to do and how to do it. Our inability to understand each other's views on life was rapidly driving us apart.

After witnessing one of our heated disputes, my sister-in-law gave me a book called *Personality Plus*, by Florence Littauer, which made us look differently at our faltering relationship. *Personality Plus* was the book that began my journey of discovery into the facets of human nature and personality – something I had never thought about until then. From *Personality Plus*, which taught us about our different temperaments, I moved on to study the Myers-Briggs Type Indicator, which taught us about our different Personality Types.

Being introduced to these personality tools was like opening Aladdin's cave. Exciting treasures were revealed in the form of new ideas that we had never thought about or applied in our daily lives. The most important idea for us was understanding that all human beings are different. Until then, we had been trying to clone ourselves and make the other person just like us – in other words, perfect! It might seem obvious, but *understanding* differences and being able to see them as *individual perspectives* – not the right way or wrong way of being in the world – are what make relationships interesting and vibrant for everyone. They provide context for why we do what we do, and how to communicate effectively with

INTRODUCTION

each other. Once Paul and I were open to this idea, we were able to begin working on re-establishing our relationship.

When my sister-in-law gave us that book about understanding personalities, she set in motion a process that changed our lives and saved our marriage. Finally we were able to recognise and understand our differences. This made me realise that I didn't really want Paul to be the life of the party – that was *my* thing. From Paul's perspective, he didn't want me constantly critiquing and questioning his plans and ideas. He was happy just sharing his knowledge. We finally knew why we were in a state of constant disagreement and we had the knowledge to do something about it.

We understood how the other person 'ticked'. Our expectations of each other changed and we decided that we would respect, although not necessarily agree with, each other's viewpoints. This new attitude gave us a chance to really look at the things that were important to us in our relationship and talk about them. We also gained greater clarity about other people's personalities and were able to bring that to our parenting once we started adding to our family.

It is important to know your own Personality Types and differences in order to keep your relationship healthy and happy. This in turn helps create a home environment that will support your number one goal as parents – your children's happiness and well-being. This is what we are going to do in Part 1.

Understanding your own personality and your partner's, particularly in times when your patience and understanding of each other is at its lowest, can help avoid serious conflict and stress.

Part 1 describes the eight different elements of the MBTI instrument as they apply in the context of a marriage or partnership.

> **Please read through the whole of Part 1 (both preferences please), then go back and tick the boxes in the checklists that you feel best apply to you and to your partner.**

WHO IS THIS MONSTER (OR TREASURE) IN MY HOUSE?

You will undoubtedly tick some of the boxes in each preference, as we can all use both preferences, but I am hoping that one will feel innately more comfortable. If not, don't worry. Write yourself some pointers about the treasures/monsters you have found in the section provided at the end.

Once you have discovered your 'diamonds', give your partner the chance to find theirs. But bear in mind that in most relationships there will be one partner who will take the lead in understanding the Type journey. If you are reading this, I am assuming that it is you, so you might need to find ways to communicate the information to your partner that will make it easy for them to be involved.

My husband, Paul, does not enjoy *reading* self-development books; however, he doesn't mind *hearing* the information. So, what I do is give him a verbal breakdown of any book or topic that I might want to discuss. He wants to know the facts, and the benefits of knowing those facts, so that he can make practical use of the information in his personal relationships – he just doesn't want to read the book. We usually do this out of the house and away from distractions, over an enjoyable coffee or brunch.

It's important for you to work out the best way for you and your partner to discuss your learnings. Once you have done this, you will be able to fill in your profiles (or guesses) at the end of the partner section.

Ready?

CHAPTER 1

EXTRAVERT OR INTROVERT PARENT/PARTNER

I'm sure you're familiar with the terms 'Extravert' and 'Introvert'. You probably think you can spot them a mile away. Extraverts are chatty, outgoing party animals and Introverts are quiet and shy. Right? Not necessarily.

It's important to realise that this is not about being well liked or your ability to talk to people and enjoy people's company. It has nothing to do with how great you are at maintaining friendships or having fun. In fact, Introverts can learn to 'extravert' and become so skilled at it that they can be mistaken for Extraverts. And Extraverts can enjoy long periods of downtime and engaging in quiet activities by themselves. The key to understanding the difference between Introverts and Extraverts is understanding energy. Which activities energise you the most? Which can deplete your energy if you are engaged in them for too long?

The **first Personality Type preference** relates to where you get your energy from:

Extraverts (E) get their energy from the external world of people and activities, and need regular interaction.

Introverts (I) get their energy from the internal world of ideas, feelings and thoughts, and need downtime.

So, where do you get your energy from?

We can use both preferences, but one will feel more comfortable and is usually our first, more natural response to a situation.

> Please read both sections about Extravert/Introvert Parents/Partners before ticking the boxes and making your decision about where you and your partner get your energy from.

THE EXTRAVERTED (E) PARENT/PARTNER

Energised by interaction in the external world

Talk – Think – Talk

The party queen.
I am an Extraverted parent. When my children were younger, I loved throwing big birthday parties for them. It was a wonderful excuse to get my friends and family together in a place where I could have hours of fun with everyone. I organised jumping castles, games, lollies and cake – everything that could make a child happy – and gleefully assumed that *everyone* would love being with me and my family, and enjoy coming to these parties as much as I loved hosting them. But it turns out my gleeful assumption was off the mark.

After attending the Myers-Briggs Personality Type course, I realised that my Extraverted need for attention and good times was not necessarily other people's 'cup of tea'. Although reflection is not one of my personality strengths, I now appreciate that many of the adults at these parties were Introverts. They stood around for hours, politely chatting, suffering sensory overload from screaming kids and loud music. Many of them must have rejoiced when my children turned eighteen and these parties stopped.

And in my oblivion to other people's differences, I had not thought about my immediate family's needs. My Introverted son, Jack, found it stressful when the other children wanted to play with his meticulously maintained toy collection, or, when he was older, his DVDs and Xbox games. He worried that the other kids would spoil or break his things. He also hated the thought of them invading the privacy of his bedroom, where he found the peace and solitude he needed. My husband, also an Introvert, disliked the thought of so many people invading his house, and having to clean up before and after they left. The chaos was too much for him. On the other hand, my daughter, the Extravert, had a ball. Her only complaint was that she had to spend time with *all* of her guests, not just her favourites.

Only after learning about Personality Types did I realise how stressed some people had been by these frequent events, but I recognised that change was necessary to ensure that everyone had a good time. Before planning the next party, I looked at these issues. The first thing I did was ensure that Jack's personal areas were out of bounds for guests. He and I discussed which toys and other items he was happy to share, and these were selected to be used by visitors.

I now empathised with Paul's stress in the weeks before a party, and made sure that we both prepared for the event together. He reminded himself that once the guests arrived, he would enjoy their company. We planned how he would get his much-needed downtime once the guests had left. Cassie was still encouraged to be social with all the guests, not just her favourites.

After learning these valuable lessons, I invited fewer people to our parties – just the tried and true family members and friends. I kept music and children's noise to a minimum and shortened the duration of the party. This gave the Introverts (and those who just didn't like parties) a chance to

> Can you or your partner relate to the need for people to be a constant in your life? And do you feel energised by being out and in the company of others?

go home earlier and re-energise. I told my Extraverted friends, and a couple of Introverted ones who love a good chat, that they were welcome to stay longer if they wanted to. The Extraverted parent had stopped and reflected on personality differences to make parties a more enjoyable experience for everyone.

Tick the boxes that best describe your preferences

Extraverted Parents/Partners often:

- ☐ Enjoy having many friends around and love to visit other people
- ☐ Plan activities that involve other people
- ☐ Dislike being alone for too long
- ☐ Like their children to bring friends home and make life fun for their friends
- ☐ Enjoy hanging out with their children's friends
- ☐ Worry if their children do not have busy social lives
- ☐ Tend to push their children (and partners) into social situations that they might not want to participate in
- ☐ Enjoy doing lots of different things and taking their family with them. They think that it is 'normal' to be involved in many activities and expect their children to enjoy those activities
- ☐ Love to be told what a great parent they are. They enjoy being in the spotlight and think that others do too
- ☐ Often take over the conversation for their children rather than allowing their children to tell their own story
- ☐ Enjoy being in a noisy/stimulating environment, as this energises them
- ☐ Verbalise their thoughts and feelings, as this helps to process them

THE INTROVERTED (I) PARENT/PARTNER

Energised by the internal world of thoughts and ideas

Think – Talk – Think

Please give me space.
My husband, Paul, is an Introvert. He is happiest at home, enjoys solitude and often spends time alone. When our children started going to school, he was reluctant to socialise with other parents. He found ways to avoid taking the children to parties and other events so that he wouldn't have to talk to a lot of strangers. Talking to people he didn't know well sapped his energy and left him exhausted. Parent-teacher interviews weren't his thing, either. He tried to avoid them by asking me to go on my own, saying I would make a much better impression upon the teacher. But I would resist this plea because he was already avoiding so many social occasions.

Paul also found it stressful when our daughter invited friends to have sleepovers at our house. Cassie and her friends tended to be noisy and chaotic. Although we gave them clear boundaries about where they could play, they usually broke these rules. We would find them building cubbies with our bedcovers, playing hide and seek under the bed and generally invading Paul's (and my) privacy. Paul preferred to wake up in his own space with his own kids' faces on the other side of the breakfast bar, not kids he didn't know.

I was aware that Paul was letting his Introversion isolate him from the children's lives. As the years went on, Cass and Jack became increasingly reliant on me attending to their social needs and taking them to events. Although I loved this, I didn't feel it was a good balance of our parenting. Paul wanted to have a close relationship with Jack and Cassie and be involved in their lives, so we talked about the changes he could make to feel comfortable in social situations. Paul was happy and comfortable to extend himself socially in familiar, smaller group settings where he could interact in a more personal way, so we focused on those. We also focused on the fact that there were others who felt the same way that

Paul did, and who would understand this stress. I was happy to attend new and unfamiliar social settings, which he found particularly daunting, on my own. We both recognised that if we could work together with our strengths, we would make a great team.

Excited to be given the chance to meet new people, and knowing that I didn't have to drag along a reluctant husband, I attended the parent-teacher interviews without Paul. I went out of my Extraverted way to impress the teachers with my friendly nature and wit. I made sure that they would love my children (and me): mission accomplished. Paul, in turn, made the effort to socialise with other parents. Doing so in small groups and on his terms made it easier and more enjoyable for him. He was also determined to get to know the children's friends when they visited. He welcomed them warmly, and asked questions about what was happening in their lives. Paul is a good listener and he loves chatting with our children's friends, and we gather from them that the feeling is mutual. Jack and Cass are also very in tune with Paul's need to escape to solitude, and are adept at moving their friends on when they sense his energy levels and interest dissipating. They appreciate the effort he has made to establish these enduring relationships with their friends – it is a credit to a man who could have chosen a different personality journey.

Recognising the need for a healthy balance between the outer world of people and inner world of thoughts can be challenging for Introverts and Extraverts. Knowing who you are and what energises you is very important to help you understand how to maintain your relationships with those you love.

Can you or your partner relate to this need for downtime from the world?

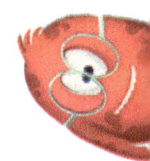

Tick the boxes that best describe your preferences

Introverted Parents/Partners often:

- Like quiet routines and are disturbed by loud, raucous behaviour and voices
- Plan activities that are centred on their immediate family, with maybe a couple of close friends included
- Prefer just one or two of their children's friends to visit for a 'play date', and will organise arrival time and drop-off to suit them so that they can re-energise after the guests leave
- Leave their children to amuse themselves – they do not see the need to entertain them
- Choose not to take their children to social settings, such as parties or playgroups, where mingling with parents they don't know might be necessary. They prefer to stay at home with their children
- Overthink incidents that affect their children, mulling over them internally without expressing their thoughts to others. By the time they speak out they are often worked up, and verbalise their thoughts inappropriately or as an attack
- Enjoy praise for parenting in a more intimate situation rather than in front of others
- Shut down if overwhelmed by conversation, and prefer small groups of other friends/parents to talk to
- Respect the privacy of others, but often appear uncommunicative to children (and partners); they do not always share or ask questions because they do not want to appear invasive
- Show their love and communication more effectively in the written form – thank goodness for texts
- Are stressed by society's expectations for their children to have many friends, sleepovers and parties
- Listen well and will give their partner or children the time to tell them their thoughts, concerns and ideas

So, where do you get your energy from?

Remember, we can use both preferences, but one will feel more comfortable and is usually our first, more natural response to a situation.

Tick the boxes

I am an:
- ○ Extravert
- ○ Introvert
- ○ Unsure

My partner is an:
- ○ Extravert
- ○ Introvert
- ○ Unsure

MBTI: E = Extravert and I = Introvert

WHO IS THIS MONSTER (OR TREASURE) IN MY HOUSE?

What Monsters/Treasures have you discovered?

Summarise your thoughts

CHAPTER 2

SENSING OR INTUITIVE PARENT/PARTNER

The second pair of preferences in the MBTI is Sensing and Intuition. Again, you probably think you know what these terms mean. We've all heard of 'women's intuition'. Maybe you think intuition is supernatural nonsense. And when it comes to sensing, what are we talking about? A sixth sense? No, not at all.

In the context of the MBTI, Sensing refers to people who like to begin their understanding of concepts and ideas at the 'bottom of the stairs' so to speak. They like to climb the stairs of learning and experience to reach the big picture at the top. Intuitive people have the big-picture vision of understanding a concept in their heads. They can already see the outcome of all of the details the Sensing people see. They are at the 'top of the steps' and, although they can step down to see the specifics of the process, they don't want to; they find it boring and a big turn-off. For example, when looking at building a house, Intuitives often see themselves sitting in the house they want to build and can describe the windows, the furnishings and the view. The Sensing people are busy getting their loans, finding a block of land, and working out which architect they're going to use. They can't see the outcome until they have taken care of the specific details.

The **second Personality Type preference** relates to the way that people take in and use information:

Sensing (S) people make sense of the world and gather information through their five senses. They enjoy details, repetition and tradition. They prefer concrete, factual information and use it to build an understanding of the bigger picture.

Intuitive (N) people gather information as patterns and connections rather than focusing on individual facts. They prefer to use their imagination, follow hunches, innovate, and enjoy abstract concepts and theories. They need to see the big picture in order to understand the parts.

So, how do you see the world?

We can use both preferences, but one will feel more comfortable and is usually our first, more natural response to a situation.

> Please read both sections about Sensing/Intuition Parents/Partners before ticking the boxes and making your decision about how you and your partner take in information.

SENSING (S) PARENT/PARTNER

Give me the details

Details – Repetition – Tradition

The inevitability of change.
I am a Sensing parent; in fact, my family all have a preference for Sensing. We use our five senses (touch, sight, smell, hearing and taste) to help us

gather information from our world. Changes that are conceptual and theoretical do not make much sense to us unless we can see the benefits in a concrete form. Innovation and change seem unnecessary to us if the process currently in place is already doing the job. We don't understand why we need to 're-invent the wheel'. Familiar processes and details keep Sensing Types in touch with reality, and create a feeling of stability and reassurance in our daily lives.

One of my favourite times of year is Christmas, and after I was married I continued the Christmas traditions of my childhood with my own family. I gave Jack and Cassie pillow cases with Santas printed on them, just like my brothers and I had. On Christmas Eve, the pillow cases would be placed on the hearth beside a Christmas stocking, waiting for Santa to stuff them full of presents for the children to discover on Christmas morning. A soft toy with chocolates waited by the children's bedroom doors as an early morning treat. As a family, we still watch our favourite Christmas movies in the evenings leading up to Christmas, even though we know every scene off by heart. We have attended the same friend's Christmas Eve party every year for twenty years. Various relatives are seen on alternate years, and have a designated time slot for the day's celebrations. We even issue clear and detailed instructions for these celebrations, maybe to the point of overdoing it! As Sensing Types, we enjoy experiencing the here and now moments that the Christmas season brings.

But my Intuitive brother feels smothered by our annual Christmas rigmarole. To him, our need to have a tangible, consistent reality is a boring process of repetition. Every year, he and I have a good-humoured debate about the value of change, and he tells me why I should do something different and let go of some of the details. I listen to his ideas about different ways of sharing Christmas with us, even though the thought of changes to the routine makes my family feel uncomfortable and stressed. His suggestions involve spending Christmas in different locations, such as the beach or a restaurant, or in other states or countries. Or finding different times to visit each other. Or having seafood for Christmas dinner instead of turkey. Maybe inviting extra people to join us. Most of his ideas are too much for me, but we have agreed to include some of his changes each Christmas. I then work out the details needed to make these 'pie in the sky' ideas happen, such as booking plane tickets and accommodation. This helps my brother feel heard and, while it causes a slight bump in the usually comfortable road of familiarity for my family, it makes way for new paths of thought and creativity.

Does the idea of throwing your routines and traditions out of the window seem difficult for you or do you enjoy creating change?

As our children have grown up and found partners, I have accepted that not all members of my immediate family can be with my husband and me on Christmas Day. We are embracing new ways of catching up with family at different times and places, and have made changes in our routines for exchanging presents. We are rolling with the changes and my brother is enjoying the variety that this brings to our family's celebrations. As our family gatherings have become more varied, I have to admit that they have also become more exciting. As Sensing Types, my family and I have had to let go of the step-by-step approach to celebrations, although Cassie was devastated when she didn't receive her teddy and chocolates this year – at the ripe old age of twenty-five! Understanding that we need 'different strokes for different folks' can cause some discomfort in the short term, but is necessary and, ultimately, rewarding.

Christmas the traditional way in the Mason household

Tick the boxes that best describe your preferences

Sensing Parents/Partners often:

- ○ Rely on 'concrete' information and want to 'see' the results or the processes; they seek experiential learning
- ○ Need to learn and do things in life using a step-by-step approach and in turn use this method to teach their children
- ○ Like details; in fact, they often plan in great detail and get bogged down in the 'small stuff', unable to see their way out
- ○ Are realists and are often seen as sensible. They see things as they are. They do not look for reasons that are out of the box or different, or that don't make sense
- ○ Live by the experiences that life brings them; they are in the here and now
- ○ Use facts and proven examples to make their decisions quickly. They would rather take care of a task now than think about something that needs future consideration
- ○ Like things in life to be sequential; one following another. They like to follow familiar patterns
- ○ Have a great memory for past and present events and situations
- ○ Prefer detailed answers to their specific questions. If they are not given the details, they will be persistent in asking for them
- ○ Prefer that their children get something done in the here and now, rather than sit around 'day dreaming'
- ○ Focus on their family's lives and well-being in the present, rather than imagining how their children or their needs fit into the bigger picture
- ○ Give clear, detailed instructions, probably to the point of overdoing it; they expect that others need these details as much as they do

THE INTUITIVE (N) PARENT/PARTNER

Give me vision and change

Big picture – Future orientated – Change maker

A different view of the world.
Intuitives are change makers and ideas people, and they keep the world in constant evolution. Their big-picture outlook on the future possibilities of life is more important to them than the details of how to get there. These can come later, if at all.

I had an interesting discussion with a friend, an Intuitive mum, about the different ways we view the world and how our views are reflected in our child rearing. She later sent me an email describing some examples of her unique parenting style:

'As a parent I broke the mould of my rigid childhood upbringing. I did everything I could to ensure that my children had fun and freedom. When they were young, I bought a wooden dining table with a thick table-top and let all members of the family draw, write, engrave and burn into its surface. The children loved it and spent hours talking about their vandalism/art. Leaving their mark on the table created a story book of their lives. Although it was not the polished fine dining table some people would prefer, it was a testament of family.

Can you relate to breaking conventional rules and traditions in innovative ways?

Nothing right or wrong. Just different!

'One of the highlights during school holidays was having the "dorm" activated. During the school term the dorm was our family study room; however, once school holidays arrived, all four children were allowed to claim the place as their own. We put spare mattresses on the floor, they added their special blankets, teddies, et cetera to their chosen beds, and selected videos and games to play. They were allowed to have water and popcorn in the room, and it was so exciting to hear them giggling, discussing, planning and then living the "dream". There was no curfew.'

My friend's family traditions are obviously in contrast to my own family, in which four Sensing Types embrace a calm, ordered life full of familiarity and predictability.

Tick the boxes that best describe your preferences

Intuitive Parents/Partners often:

- O   Appear a bit vague in conversation and in relation to ideas
- O   Enjoy the chance to use their imagination and design their own things, whether it is parties, play costumes, games, holidays or even stories; they will often create their own bedtime stories, much to the delight of their children
- O   Get stressed having to follow detailed steps towards a goal. They prefer to start by picturing the result of their actions
- O   Dismiss deadlines if their desire for change/innovation can't be accommodated
- O   Regard time as endless – they do not sit in the moment but look to the future
- O   Find that the future can be a source of worry as they wonder about what the world will be like when their children grow up
- O   Use their vision to become the world's greatest 'reasoners' and give a positive perspective on things that otherwise appear bleak and hopeless
- O   See the big picture rather than get caught up in the detail of the moment; they can often see a way of solving problems and moving forward that others might not
- O   Believe that they can always do more and that there is always more to life, and want to explore this
- O   Build big pictures and solutions – they will give you the whole package
- O   Intuitively pick up on people's emotions and situations that might not be obvious to others
- O   Love to brainstorm when solving problems

So, how do you take in information?
Remember that we can use both preferences, but one will feel more comfortable and is usually our first, more natural response to a situation.

Tick the boxes

I am:
- ○ Sensing
- ○ Intuitive
- ○ Unsure

My partner is:
- ○ Sensing
- ○ Intuitive
- ○ Unsure

MBTI: S = Sensing and N = Intuitive

NOTE: N is used for Intuitive as there is already an I (Introvert) on the MBTI profile.

WHO IS THIS MONSTER (OR TREASURE) IN MY HOUSE?

What Monsters/Treasures have you discovered?

Summarise your thoughts

CHAPTER 3

THINKING OR FEELING PARENT/PARTNER

Thinking and Feeling are the next pair of glorious opposites in the MBTI system. So that's brainiacs and cry babies, right? No, of course not; we all have feelings and we can all think.

The term 'thinking' is not the same as intelligence. The term 'feeling' is not the same as emotion. I am a Feeling Type; this does not mean that I can't think! My family are all Thinking Types; this does not mean that they can't feel! The words used in this context refer to the way that we make our decisions, using either our *logic* or our *values* in our initial reaction to a situation. When my husband and I interview people for jobs, he is looking for the logical criteria: skills, resumes, references, experience. I am looking for someone who will fit in with the team, and who is kind and caring. This does not necessarily affect what we finally decide. If we went with Paul's ideal person, we might end up with someone with no people skills. If we looked purely at my choices, we might end up with a lovely person with no skills at all for the job. So a blend of the two preference choices usually works. The terms Thinking and Feeling, in the context of the MBTI, refer to the criteria that we look at *first* when making decisions. However, we may use both of our preferences to make our *final* decision.

The **third Personality Type preference** relates to how people form their decisions (their decision-making process):

Thinking (T) Thinking Types seek *logical* reasons in making their decisions. They are usually firm and fair, seek honesty and look at consequences. They ask 'Why?'

Feeling (F) Feeling Types use their *values* to make their decisions. They pursue harmonious relationships, consider the impact of their decisions on people and like to be appreciated. They ask 'Who?'

So, how do you make your decisions?

We can use both preferences, but one will feel more comfortable and is usually our first, more natural response to a situation.

> Please read both sections about Thinking/Feeling Parents/Partners before ticking the boxes and making your decision about how you and your partner form decisions.

THE THINKING (T) PARENT/PARTNER

How can we fix that?

Logic – Reasoning – Fair

Looking at the other side.
My husband, Paul, is always thinking! He uses the words, 'You would think...' constantly in his conversation and yes, he is a Thinking Type. His thoughts are critiquing and logical. He is continually looking to right any wrongs that he sees, or rather perceives, and will inform people bluntly about the things that need to be fixed.

I remember the time we ran an MBTI workshop with our managers to find out more about each other and how we worked together as a team. During the session, we had a revealing discussion with our managers about how Thinking Types and Feeling Types interpret emails.

Paul discovered that the Feeling Types were upset by the tone of the emails he sent. These emails went along the lines of...

'John, the pumps need fixing by Saturday.

Paul'

The Thinking Type managers could not see anything wrong with this very straightforward message. It was clear in its meaning, and there was no need for emotion or personal warmth – there was a job to be done, so just do it. They valued the simplicity of Paul's message and the absence of emotive language because it appealed to their preference for logic and reasoning. However, we all like to be shown some appreciation from time to time, regardless of what Type we are, so a simple 'Thanks' would have been a good addition.

But the Feeling Types who received messages like this wanted more warmth in the language. They like to understand that they are being thought of at a more personal level. For example...

'Hi John,

I hope that you had a great weekend and the family are well.

The pumps are currently not working. Could you please get them fixed by Friday?

Your help is much appreciated.

Thanks,
Paul'

Do you find it feels unnatural to make warm, 'fuzzy' comments to people?

This was an eye opener for everyone in the workshop about the differences in the expectations and thoughts of the Feeling and Thinking Types. It showed us all how important these personality tools are in communication. He didn't really like it, but Paul saw the value in this feedback and took it on board. He now makes an effort to thank everyone, and put feeling and emotion into his emails when writing to the Feeling staff members. It is a stressful process for him, and he does have to ask for my help when writing these emails because the feeling words don't flow naturally. Nonetheless, he is willing to put the time into building harmonious relationships with our staff.

Tick the boxes that best describe your preferences

Thinking Parents/Partners often:

- ○ View discipline as what is fair and reasonable
- ○ Dislike being drawn into emotional responses; they may feel locked in and become angry and uncomfortable if their logical, analytical approach is not understood or respected
- ○ Are more likely to be moved by a logical argument from their children about an issue at hand, rather than by the children's emotional response
- ○ Use logical language and will appear to critique anything that is said or done
- ○ Ask 'Why?' when their children do something that they might not approve of or want to participate in, and require a logical answer
- ○ Debate any subject; whether they agree or not, they love the chance to question and explore ideas
- ○ Have rules and principles around household chores, tasks and discipline, although they will not always follow them through
- ○ Appear task focused, and like competence and efficiency
- ○ Encourage competence, independence and critical thinking
- ○ Argue their own point of view, and do not always negotiate with their children if they think that they are in the right
- ○ Appear intolerant and dismissive of their children's ideas if they disagree with them
- ○ Feel it is not necessary to comment on the positives in their children's lives, such as receiving an A for an assignment, as these are obvious. They would rather spend time on the improvements, and are more likely to say, 'How can you get an A+ next time?'

THE FEELING (F) PARENT/ PARTNER

Are you okay?

Values - Harmony – Empathy

Walking in the footsteps of others.
Many years ago, when my children were eight and ten years old, we were on a family picnic at a park and were all watching a toddler attempt to climb the biggest slippery dip in the nearby playground. To our horror, he fell down the steps, and as he lay crying I noted our responses: Mine was, 'Oh my goodness! Poor child - I hope he is okay.' I was concerned that he might be injured and that his caregiver had not noticed. My first instinct was to start running towards him. However, my Thinking family's response was quite different! Almost in unison, they said, 'He shouldn't have been climbing that high, and where is his mother?' Paul added, 'Don't go over. His mother will be around somewhere - it's her responsibility to look after him.' How unfeeling, I thought. My heart was in my mouth with concern over this poor child's well-being. However, my family's comments were logical and true. I did not have to go and 'rescue' the child, as his mother did appear very quickly when she heard his cries. I should point out that my family did follow up their initial comments with concerns such as, 'I hope he is okay', but their first response was not the emotional one. I too, in retrospect, questioned the safety measures and height of the play equipment and where the child's caregiver was, but, again, it was not my immediate thought.

It was then that I realised that logical thinking is always going to be at the forefront of my family's thoughts. For each of them, their first thought is 'Why?' As a Feeling Type, my first thought is 'Who?' My family's feeling thoughts are also there and can be reached, but it may take a bit of digging to bring their empathy and sensitivity to the surface. I have also learned that my ability to feel instantly empathetic, and my desire to look after others at an emotional level, can make my Thinking family feel overwhelmed, uncomfortable and cynical.

The incident in the park was a turning point for me in my understanding of Thinking Types. I realised that, as I was living with them 24/7, I had to put myself in my family's shoes when looking at decision making and other thought processes. I learned to change my reaction to their thinking language and understand it for what it was - not mean or hurtful, just logical, critiquing and straightforward. This enabled me to become resilient towards their language, and empathetic to their thoughts and those of other Thinking Types I meet as I move through life. I consider myself lucky to have had the chance to learn this valuable lesson. It has brought me much emotional relief, and released me from my expectations of others. I am a much happier and more well-balanced person as a result. Although I don't usually agree with how they go about things, I now 'get' my family's decision-making process.

Can you relate to using 'why' or 'who' to make decisions about people?

Remember, we can use both preferences and one can follow the other very quickly.

My three Thinkers and me

Tick the boxes that best describe your preferences

Feeling Parents/Partners often:

- ○ Expect that their children will share their values around people and relationships
- ○ Encourage their children to think about others in their decision making
- ○ Point out things that they like about people and look for the good, rather than critique the negative
- ○ Make excuses for others' shortcomings and look at the circumstances surrounding them
- ○ Want to be recognised for being caring and looking after their children's as well as their friends' emotional well-being
- ○ Use emotive language that appeals to a Feeling person's natural mode of decision making
- ○ Give children another chance when rules are broken if they feel that there are mitigating circumstances
- ○ Avoid conflict, and will give in to demands and tolerate certain behaviours, if it will bring about harmony
- ○ Find that the approval of their children and partner is of utmost importance for their happiness
- ○ Sacrifice their own time/happiness in order to help or support their children
- ○ Provide verbal and physically demonstrative support for their children in a sensitive and nurturing manner
- ○ Encourage cooperation, empathy and concern for others

So, how do you make decisions?
Remember that we can use both preferences, but one will feel more comfortable and is usually our first, more natural response to a situation.

THINKING OR FEELING PARENT/PARTNER

Tick the boxes

I am:
- ○ Feeling
- ○ Thinking
- ○ Unsure

My partner is an:
- ○ Feeling
- ○ Thinking
- ○ Unsure

MBTI: F = Feeling and T = Thinking

WHO IS THIS MONSTER (OR TREASURE) IN MY HOUSE?

What Monsters/Treasures have you discovered?

Summarise your thoughts

CHAPTER 4

JUDGING OR PERCEIVING PARENT/PARTNER

Nobody likes to be called judgemental. But when we talk about being a Judging Type in the MBTI, we're not talking about looking down our noses at people or judging others. When we talk about Perceiving Types, we are not looking at how people use their perception to judge people, either. This pair of preferences is about how people like to live. Judging Types do like order and structure, and at their worst they can appear controlling and over the top in their desire for perfection. Perceiving Types control their world by adapting to events as they occur. They are often able to work in messy environments and enjoy acting spontaneously. Perceiving does not indicate laziness, but at their worst Perceiving Types can be terrible procrastinators.

The **fourth Personality Type preference** relates to how people live their outer lives (their lifestyle):

Judging (J) Judging Types prefer an outer life that has structure and order, and they like to make decisions and choices quickly so that they can have closure. They would agree with the motto: 'Just Do It' … according to a fixed plan.

Perceiving (P) Perceiving Types prefer an outer life that is more flexible and enjoy exploring options that give them room for spontaneity, just in case something else comes up. They would agree with the motto: 'Let's wait and see.'

So, how do you like to live your outer life?

Remember that we are all able to use both preferences, but one will feel more comfortable and is likely to be our first, more natural response to a situation.

> Please read both sections about Judging/Perceiving Parents/Partners before ticking the boxes and making your decision about how you and your partner live your outer lives.

THE JUDGING (J) PARENT/PARTNER

Just do it!

Planned – Structured – Organised

Too much preparation?
When preparing for her first child, my Judging Type friend, Rebecca, made sure she was organised. She researched everything, bought the appropriate furnishings and educational toys for her newborn, and prepared her house in advance by making sure that she would have a child-safe environment when her baby became mobile. She chose the best healthcare plan to ensure that she and her baby would be well cared for on the medical front. She even went as far as to put her name on the list for the schools she wanted to send her child to. Confident that everything was all worked out for at least the first twelve months of her child's life, Rebecca

packed her hospital bag a month before her due date and waited.

When Rebecca's son, James, was born, she was quick to establish routines and boundaries, and create good habits and behaviours. This would help to ensure that, as he grew, he felt secure. James was also expected to be well behaved, both at home and in public. A checklist was kept, ensuring that he was meeting his developmental milestones. Sleep and playtime were scheduled throughout the day and rarely altered.

But, as we all know, children don't always do things by the book. Rebecca struggled to keep order and control as she battled the uncertainty and unpredictability that having a child brings to your life. She often felt overwhelmed and exhausted by trying to live up to her own high expectations.

Rebecca's Perceiving Type sister offered to babysit when James was nine months old. When Rebecca came home after her night out, she found her sister and son rolling around on the floor and giggling together. Dishes were in the sink, toys were thrown everywhere, and James was chewing on Rebecca's old teddy bear (which she had put on a high shelf, for safe keeping, in her son's room).

Rebecca was horrified by the situation when she walked in and had to resist the urge to immediately 'fix' everything. But as she sat and watched her sister's interaction with James, seeing the joy on his face as he sucked on the teddy's ear and rolled around on the crumb-covered floor, she reflected on the stress she was putting herself under in order to chase her goal of having a happy, healthy baby. She could see that her house and her own behaviour did not always need to be perfect. She was allowing her personal need for order and structure to interfere with many opportunities for real fun and closeness. With this insight, she was able to slowly let go of many of her fixed expectations – but not all of them! These days, Rebecca spends many unstructured hours relaxing, playing and cuddling with James for the pure enjoyment of being together.

As parents, we never stop learning!

Tick the boxes that best describe your preferences

Judging Parents/Partners often:

○ Like order and structure, some more than others
○ Find diaries, timetables, schedules and lists very important in the smooth running of daily life. If they do not carry their planner, they have it in their heads
○ Find that changing pre-scheduled events and details causes great frustration and annoyance, as they have their day/week/year planned in advance and often set in stone
○ Expect that others will also have planned schedules and times, and are appalled by people who don't. Work has a plan to be followed, as do holidays
○ Plan holidays and activities well in advance, sometimes up to a year
○ Feel unsettled until they have reached a conclusion and will finalise a decision as quickly as possible
○ Have excellent planning skills for future events, either at work or at home. For example, workplace commitments, travel, et cetera
○ Implement punishment immediately if children behave badly, rather than waiting to see if the behaviour improves or if there are mitigating circumstances
○ Rarely change their minds about discipline as they are very good at 'sticking to their guns'
○ Can put unrealistic time frames/bans on their children
○ Develop great skills in time management. They expect people to be on time and committed to promises/appointments
○ Enjoy planning and organising parties and events

THE PERCEIVING (P) PARENT/PARTNER

Let's wait and see

Flexible – Adaptable – Spontaneous

Listen to our children.
As parents we usually think that we know what is best for our children, so we don't tend to listen closely to their complaints. I worked with a couple of easy-going Perceiving parents who did not want to put too many deadlines or structures into their children's lives. They preferred a sense of flow and assumed that this was right for their children too. How wrong they were.

Their flexible approach drove their Judging son, Nick, to distraction. He told them about his frustration, but they ignored him and continued to follow their preferred way of parenting because it felt comfortable and normal to them. When I sat down with Nick and his parents, he reiterated his stresses. He explained, again, how upset he was when last-minute decisions were made without allowing him time to prepare for the required changes to his personal schedule. His parents' casual attitude to their responsibilities around his schooling – such as getting him to school on time (his time), having diaries signed, returning notices before the final request and attending parent meetings – made him feel like they did not care about either his schooling or him. Nick was in a state of constant stress, unable to plan ahead or organise his daily life.

Nick's anger and distress about his parents' indifference to his need for punctuality was an eye opener for them. But by learning about their different Types, Nick and his parents were able to understand and share their different points of view. His parents explained that they had good intentions and had not wanted to be too uptight or stress Nick by putting high expectations on him. In turn, Nick was able to help them understand his side of the personality story. He explained that their actions were stressing him more, not less, and explained what would help him feel less stressed. Time management was a high priority for him. Being punctual, or even early, at all times, but especially for school drop-off, was heaven for him. Getting anything that required a signature handed in as early as possible felt right. Knowing that his mum and dad would attend meetings for parents, even though they might think that they knew what was happening at school, made him feel cared for. Letting him know in advance, whenever possible, about changes to schedules that involved him would make him feel more secure.

Personality behaviours can be complicated if you don't recognise the type of personality driving the behaviours early on. Different, but satisfying, solutions can be found when you truly listen to the people you love.

Nick's parents were shocked at how different their perception of being great parents was from their son's. They were more than prepared to start making changes to their own behaviours and look at things from his perspective. But this was not an overnight fix. Changing from your preferred way of doing things to something that feels less natural takes thought and resolution. But in their acknowledgement of how important these things were for him, Nick started to feel heard and more able to forgive and forget when his parents occasionally 'stuffed up'. He knew it was a two-way street, and that he had to give and take as well.

Tick the boxes that best describe your preferences

Perceiving Parents/Partners often:

- ○ Have a 'to-do' list or several, but usually lose them, forget to finish them or leave them at home
- ○ Are adaptable to change. They will allow children to change their minds without too much discord, unless they are under time stress
- ○ Seize the moment and enjoy doing things that are not necessarily on their 'schedule'
- ○ Find it easy to put jobs, chores or 'life' off until tomorrow
- ○ Are caught running around in the morning, ironing clothes or finishing chores that they should have done the night before. It is okay, as they work best when under last-minute pressure
- ○ Leave 'puddles' of jobs and work around the house that they have started but not finished. They will all be done in good time, just not now
- ○ Change plans to include extra things that pop up in their day
- ○ Feel energised by last-minute pressure, and enjoy helping out in the moment
- ○ Find plans and time-framed commitments off-putting
- ○ Can do several things at once and, when it comes to finishing them, will complete the one with the earliest deadline first
- ○ Upset others by changing plans at the last minute
- ○ Are late for appointments (although usually only by a few minutes ☺)

So, how do you live your outer life?
Remember that we can use both preferences, but one will feel more comfortable and is usually our first, more natural response to a situation.

Tick the boxes

I am an:
- ◯ Perceiving
- ◯ Judging
- ◯ Unsure

My partner is an:
- ◯ Perceiving
- ◯ Judging
- ◯ Unsure

MBTI: P = Perceiving and J = Judging

JUDGING OR PERCEIVING PARENT/PARTNER

What Monsters/Treasures have you discovered?

Summarise your thoughts

PART 1

ACTION: SUMMARISE YOUR PERSONALITY TYPE

Now go back to each preference that you identified for yourself and your partner in each of the boxed areas at the end of each chapter in Part 1. You can find the results on the following pages:

E/I: page 23
S/N: page 33
T/F: page 43
J/P: page 52

List the four Personality Types (for example, INTJ) that you think you and your partner might be:

Your Personality Type Profile: _____

Your Partner's Personality Type Profile: _____

Your selected letters now form one of the sixteen MBTI profiles. This valuable combination of your preferences will help you discover and recognise your potential strengths and areas of development. It will give you an increasing awareness of the differences between Types and show you how to value those who think and act differently from you.

ISTJ	ISFJ	INFJ	INTJ
ISTP	ISFP	INFP	INTP
ESTP	ESFP	ENFP	ENTP
ESTJ	ESFJ	ENFJ	ENTJ

You and your partner will now have a picture of your differences and similarities in each of the four preference areas. Identifying your Type profiles will open the door to further discussion and greater empathy for each other's views on life.

Remember, however, that your personality profile is a work in progress. You may find, as you go through this book and do further research, that your initial preference choices might change. If your profile does not 'feel' right, try changing one of the areas that was a very close second when choosing your Type preferences.

Much of the time, we want other people to be more like us. After all, we are pretty cool. But learning about personalities helps us to become more aware of others and what is important to them. This knowledge opens our eyes and hearts to welcome the treasures that other people can bring into our lives.

PART 2

FINDING THE PERSONALITY 'JEWELS' IN YOUR CHILD/CHILDREN

In Part 1, I described how my relationship with my husband began to deteriorate as the first flush of romance wore off. How the treasures we found in each other soon became monsters. It was discovering and learning about different personality tools, in particular the MBTI, that I believe ultimately saved my marriage. It also helped us on our parenting journey. And while it wasn't all smooth sailing, I firmly believe that without my knowledge of Personality Types, I would never have been able to find the treasures that were waiting to be discovered in my little monsters.

Jack, my firstborn, was for the most part an easy child. He was so ordered and organised that I rarely saw any tantrums or emotive outbursts from him. He was calm and patient and very easily bribed, which worked well for both of us! I just seemed to have this great kid, and I thought I must have been the most amazing mother. Of course, as he grew older, I was able to identify his Type, and realised that much of the reason he was so orderly and obedient was because, as an ISTJ, order and routine were very much his cup of tea.

Of course, it wasn't all a bed of roses. There were times when Jack became stressed and angry, usually when he felt rushed by a last-minute dash somewhere or instant changes of plan. Again, typical reactions from an

ISTJ, which I got better at managing as I learned more about Types. Jack can still feel like that today, but we all recognise the triggers and can control them much better. Knowing that Jack felt secure with boundaries, clear schedules and routine helped Paul and I to be aware of our own unscheduled behaviours and make an effort to take Jack's preferences into account. Jack's parents and sister are all Perceiving Types, and he could have been one messed up child, living in a house full of last-minute people, but our knowledge of personalities guided us all. He understands who we are and appreciates the efforts we make to meet on middle ground with his time frames. We all believe that we can solve any problems with a logical, pragmatic discussion.

Although Jack didn't bring many friends home during his school years, he now shares his friends with us. He has retained his school friendships and his friends are frequent visitors to our house. As an Introvert, Jack has the skills and warmth to make friends with ease. I must have done something right!

Knowing about Type also gave me the gift of being able to calm down my overwhelming Extravert side and listen to my son. Given time and space, Jack talked and talked. He shared many things with me that he did not share with others, and I always knew who he was and trusted him implicitly. He has become a lovely, caring young man, who has great emotional intelligence and makes me laugh every day.

Of course, Jack's sister, Cassie, as an ESTP, was a different story! She was outgoing, friendly, very vocal in her agreement or disagreement with certain matters and could not be bribed in any shape or form. She just did what she wanted. After calm, Introverted Jack, she was a real shock to the system, and I realised that my Mother of the Year Award was down the tubes. I could not understand how two children, whom we tried to treat the same way, were so different. That is, until I learned about different personalities, identified my children's, and was able to treat them in the way they needed to be treated – as individuals who brought their own treasures and monsters to the table.

Knowing Cassie's Type gave me such an insight into how to handle her personality – her need for many friends, her sharp eye for details, the loud voice that told us whether she was happy or sad and the trail of clothing, toys and food that she left around the house and drove me to distraction.

In fact, I was not always a neat and tidy person myself, and I loved people just as much as Cassie did, which helped me realise she was not so different from me. I resolved to embrace her more chaotic, yet friendly, personality. I welcomed her friends with open arms and made myself the fun mum. I allowed her flexibility with going out and finishing her chores and other commitments. I knew that if I set a deadline, her situation or plans would change. With her, it was really wait and see. We both love to talk, so I kept talking and communicating with her. This was our connection, and she told me everything. I withheld judgement and was rewarded with trust. She was a remarkable teenager and today is a beautiful, emotionally intelligent young woman whom I talk to several times a day.

Knowing about and understanding personalities made my parenting journey smoother. And the fact that Paul was right beside me, learning about personalities just as I was, made us a great parenting team. Our acquired ability to recognise each other's personality differences helped us both to adjust to the 'new normal' of being parents (and parents of a premature baby). We discovered that successful parenting involves being true to your innate personality. Paul and I encouraged each other to utilise our particular strengths. This allowed us to sift through the well-meant advice from family and friends, and apply what worked best for us as parents.

One of the most important aspects of Paul's and my continuing parental journey is knowing each other's gifts and limitations. Recognising when to stay out or step in when dealing with our children. Letting go of our own judgements of how parenting should be. Understanding that because we are so different, there are other ways of parenting that could be just as good, or possibly better, than ours.

But that's enough about me! Now let's look at those children of yours…

In the following chapters, each Personality Type is explored, with personal anecdotes to assist your understanding of the Type that your child/children might be. This is a guide to use as your child develops. Many children are easily identifiable at an early age. You will be able to see and understand many of the things that make them tick. As they mature, you will see different facets of Type come into play. Their true Type will be recognisable when they are old enough to understand and acknowledge, personally, which Personality Type they might be.

Let's go!

CHAPTER 5

EXTRAVERT OR INTROVERT CHILD

The **first Personality Type preference** we will be looking at relates to where your child gets their *energy* from:

Extraverted (E) children gain energy from focusing on the external world of people and activities, and they light up in social situations. Their batteries get charged when there is a variety of discussion and interaction with other people.

Introverted (I) children get their energy from the internal world. They are energised by some time alone and quiet reflection. They are reserved and will not usually divulge private details until they get to know you. Introversion has nothing to do with shyness, lack of social skills or dislike of people – it is all to do with energy.

So, where does your child get his/her energy from?

What happens when they are unable to tap into their preference for Introversion or Extraversion?

Remember, children can use *both* preferences, but one will feel more comfortable and is usually their first, more natural response to a situation.

> **Please read both the Extravert and Introvert child sections before ticking the boxes. (If you have multiple children, perhaps use a different coloured pen for each child.)**

THE INTROVERTED (I) CHILD

Think – Talk – Think

The wisdom of youth.
When my son, Jack, was a youngster, he was often reluctant to entertain the children that I 'kindly' invited over for him to play and hang out with. I would oversee these occasions and ensure that all went to plan, even though Jack was often disgruntled about it. Afterwards, he would retire to his bedroom or the lounge room to enjoy the relaxing comfort of a video or, in later years, computer games. Obviously, I had not quite got the hang of this Type gig yet. One day, when Jack was thirteen, I tried to organise some of his friends to come over and he gently took me aside, sat me down and said with great wisdom for his age, 'Mum, I am not you; I do not need people around all the time. I see my friends at school and that is enough for me. I am very happy in my own space at home!'

How lucky was I to have a child who could not only verbalise his needs, but also recognise my need, as an Extravert, to see him surrounded by friends? A caring mother, I took this information on board and let go of my fear that he would have no friends. Jack in turn was very grateful for the recognition of his values and feelings. My concerns that Jack would have no friends were unfounded.

My 'devilish' Introverted son Jack

With me as his mother, he was always exposed to the Extraverted world and this helped him learn to socialise and communicate with others very well. My job was done. Jack does not feel uncomfortable with other people and makes friends with ease. He maintains his many friendships effortlessly, by communicating and socialising on his terms and in his preferred comfort zone.

Over to you now. Your turn… tick the boxes if you think your child displays any of the following preferences.

What have you noticed about your child?

Do they enjoy their own space and time?

Tick the boxes that you think best describe your child/children's preferences

Introverted children often:

- ○ Enjoy playing or studying on their own or with a few others
- ○ Like to think about what they are going to say before they say it
- ○ Are usually quiet around other people until they get to know them
- ○ Get tired when doing things with other people for a long time
- ○ Are re-energised from time alone
- ○ Think slowly, then act. However, if action is not required, may fail to follow through
- ○ Take time to embrace new situations, ideas and thoughts
- ○ Have a small circle of friends and often one best friend
- ○ Do not like to be the centre of attention
- ○ Do not like to be rushed when thinking through ideas and will only answer if they're sure
- ○ Can't talk about/share their feelings when upset, angry or embarrassed
- ○ Often enjoy dressing up, as being in disguise lets them become someone else

THE EXTRAVERTED (E) CHILD

Talk – Think – Talk

Spreading the love.

In contrast to Jack, my Extraverted daughter, Cassie, is stimulated by people and actions in the external world, and enjoys sharing ideas and information with anyone who will listen. She loved having her friends around to play when she was a child. At ten years of age, I overheard her telling my Introverted brother that she was having one of her 'best friends' for a sleepover. My brother is always amused by Cassie's confidence and seemingly endless conversation, and when she paused for breath he astutely asked, 'How long has she been your best friend?' 'Oh, two weeks,' Cassie replied. He shook his head and grinned, saying, 'Cassie, only you could have made a best friend in two weeks.' Becoming best friends with somebody in just two weeks was beyond comprehension for an Introvert, who needs time to make friends whom they value and trust. As he left, my brother looked at me, winked and said, 'Let me know how long that friendship lasts.' As it turned out, that child was no longer on the friendship list six weeks later; other friends had been found along the way who were more compatible.

My Extraverted daughter and her friends

Extraverts' friendships might be regarded as shallower than those of Introverts, but this is not true; it is the perception of our differences. Extraverts simply enjoy the company of many people. They are social butterflies who spread their friendship among a wide variety of companions. This element of their personality may not be appreciated by their Introverted friends, who prefer more one-on-one time in their friendships and may feel left out or ignored by this behaviour. Therefore, Introverted friendships may not last the distance with Extraverts. Other Extraverts are usually okay with this style of friendship, however, as they too enjoy having an extensive group of friends.

What have you noticed about your child?

Do they feel comfortable engaging with people and sharing their personal story?

Tick the boxes that you think best describe your child/children's preferences

Extraverted children often:

- Enjoy talking. In fact, they sometimes like to talk just to hear the sound of their own voice
- Like to talk with others to exchange ideas and information. Studying with friends is really important, but staying on track with study also needs to be addressed when this occurs
- Enjoy some background noise while working; too much quietness feels depressing and boring
- Need to verbalise everything: ideas, emotions, thoughts
- Can get into trouble for talking too much. Can be annoying in the classroom when group listening and quiet time are required
- Find sitting and listening boring and will often become restless and inattentive
- Tell you their whole story, often without being asked, and are happy to give out any information about themselves and other people if you enquire
- Enjoy having lots of friends and can befriend people quickly, but can also churn through friends swiftly
- Can appear insincere in their need for friends and how easily they gather them
- Treasure their friendships but sometimes 'spread' themselves too thinly for some, and these friends can drop off the radar
- Can have a best friend, but usually have several
- Learn best through interaction

WHO IS THIS MONSTER (OR TREASURE) IN MY HOUSE?

Refer back to the statements that you ticked and decide which Type best describes your child/ children.

(I have provided options for three children. You may need to write your own for additional children.)

Tick the most suitable box:

- ○ My child is an Extravert (E)
- ○ My child is an Introvert (I)
- ○ I am unsure

- ○ My child is an Extravert (E)
- ○ My child is an Introvert (I)
- ○ I am unsure

- ○ My child is an Extravert (E)
- ○ My child is an Introvert (I)
- ○ I am unsure

MBTI: E = Extravert and I = Introvert

Moments when you realise that there are no monsters – just buried treasures waiting to be found.

Summarise your thoughts

CHAPTER 6

SENSING OR INTUITIVE CHILD

The **second Personality Type preference** that we will be looking at relates to the way that your child/children take in information:

Sensing (S) children gather information through their five senses. They prefer concrete, factual information and use it to build an understanding of the bigger picture. They like details, repetition and tradition.

Intuitive (N) children gather their information using patterns and connections, and need to see the big picture in order to understand the parts. They like to use their imagination and create new ideas and projects. They are comfortable in the world of concepts and theories.

Where does your child get their information from?

Do they seem to be rooted in the here and now world of today, or do they prefer to let their imagination soar and explore new possibilities?

Remember, children can use both preferences, but one will feel more natural to them and is usually their first response to a situation.

> Please read both the Sensing/ Intuitive child sections before ticking the boxes. (For multiple children, perhaps use a different coloured pen for each child.)

THE SENSING (S) CHILD

Details – Repetition – Step up

Junior school writer's block.
My grade four teacher often asked us to use our imagination (either that or she hadn't planned anything to teach that day!). I remember the day she said, 'Today, I want you to write a story about anything that you want.' My instant reaction was, 'Really – anything?' This was terrifying for me. How would I write a story with no direction? I needed specifics; concrete examples to help me link my ideas to a broad, random concept. Where was the information that I, as a Sensing child, needed? So I asked, 'Can we write a story about our weekend?' 'Sure, anything you like,' was my teacher's reply. Her response really stressed me out.

When I looked over at my Intuitive friend, Tracy, I could see that she was 'on fire', intently writing her inspired story at breakneck speed. She was focused and excited by the possibilities of being able to explore unlimited topic options. Unfortunately, it would be obvious if I tried to copy her work! I put my hand up again, 'Can we write a fairy story?' I received the same answer. By now, I was stumped and could not write anything at all. My teacher finally offered me a 'hook' to hang my ideas from. 'Okay, write a story about your weekend, about going to the beach.' Oh, the relief! I now had a baseline to get me started. Once I had begun my story-writing journey, I was able use my imagination and get creative.

As a mature Sensing person, I am aware that the big picture is important at times, but I still need a 'hook' on which to hang my ideas. Understanding your child's information-gathering process, whether they be Sensing or Intuitive, is important. Conceptual ideas and theories can be difficult for the Sensing child. Help them by starting with what they know before moving forward with new and creative ideas.

What have you noticed about your child?

Do they enjoy the comfort of knowing the details and sequencing of new situations?

Tick the boxes that you think best describe your child/children's preferences

Sensing children often:

- ○ Like detailed information and lots of it. The more details they have, the clearer the idea becomes
- ○ Like clear, straightforward directions
- ○ Need to know *what to do* and *how to do it*. Without this information they are lost and find it difficult to know where to start
- ○ Like experiential learning – they learn by doing
- ○ Like to learn … practise … and learn again. This helps them retain their learning. Repetition and experience is important to understanding. This does not only apply to schoolwork. It might be learning to tie shoelaces or tidying up their rooms
- ○ Like to re-visit knowledge or learnings in order to prove that they still know the topic well
- ○ Enjoy going with an idea that has previously been covered, whether a project, story or plan, rather than being left to invent or create the idea
- ○ Like information presented to them in order, whether it is 'work' or 'play'; they are sequential thinkers and consecutive instruction is very important to them
- ○ Need to know all of the facts about the topic in hand to understand the whole idea
- ○ Use examples to help them visualise and become inspired about what they are doing. Focus on and can remember details, to the extent that they can become almost boring to talk to
- ○ See home as a haven, where traditions, ceremonies and routines are observed

THE INTUITIVE (N) CHILD

Dream – Imagine – Big picture

The Fairy Princess.
Sara was what her mother called a whimsical child. Ever since she was very young, she loved to dress up in costumes. They did not have to be shop-bought or perfect, and she would make them herself out of curtains, sheets, cardboard – anything she could find that could help create the fantasy of being another person. She had many imaginary friends, one of which was a pony called Flicker. She rode Flicker around the house and the yard each morning and groomed and fed him every day. After Flicker came myriad other imaginary friends who kept her company for much of her childhood.

Sara also loved to peer through a hole in the fence so that she could watch the neighbours, imagine what was happening in their lives and make up stories about them. She was inspired by an art show that she watched on TV about homes for toys, so she made homes for everything in her toy collection out of any materials that she could lay her hands on. Sara also loved to write stories and paint. She was excellent at both activities and often won awards at school for works that used her amazingly creative imagination. She may sound like an odd child, even perhaps one who failed to 'fit in', but her Intuitive mother and father saw all of her childhood quirks as gifts to be nourished and cherished. They fostered her Intuitive creativity, and today Sara is an artist and writer, and runs a successful children's party business that specialises in fairy themes. She is, of course, the Fairy Princess.

What have you noticed about your child?

Do they enjoy activities that use their imagination and creative skills?

Tick the boxes that you think best describe your child/children's preferences

Intuitive children often:

- ○ Are drawn to theory, patterns and the connection of ideas
- ○ Lose interest and become impatient if they can't see the big picture and are tied down to details and unconnected facts
- ○ Dislike repetitive learning and going over already taught/learned material
- ○ Are highly imaginative, and enjoy games and activities that use their imagination and creative ideas
- ○ Learn about many different things in diverse ways
- ○ Prefer minimal directions so that they can do what needs to be done their way. Inventing ideas is fun!
- ○ Like to know the central focus of an idea and may miss the details
- ○ Are often 'ideas people', and enjoy the end result rather than the process of actually making or producing their invention!
- ○ Need limited examples to illustrate a point. Otherwise, they lose interest quickly; boredom will take over
- ○ Enjoy doing things in a different way from others. They like to use their creativity and ideas to make their work special
- ○ Spend a lot of time daydreaming
- ○ Have imaginary friends

Refer back to the statements that you ticked and decide which Type best describes your child/ children.

(I have provided options for three children. You may need to write your own for additional children.)

Tick the most suitable box:

- ○ My child is Sensing (S)
- ○ My child is Intuitive (N)
- ○ I am unsure

- ○ My child is Sensing (S)
- ○ My child is Intuitive (N)
- ○ I am unsure

- ○ My child is Sensing (S)
- ○ My child is Intuitive (N)
- ○ I am unsure

MBTI: S = Sensing and N = Intuitive

NOTE: N is used for Intuitive as there is already an I (Introvert) on the MBTI profile.

WHO IS THIS MONSTER (OR TREASURE) IN MY HOUSE?

Moments when you realise that there are no monsters – just buried treasures waiting to be found.

Summarise your thoughts

_____
_____
_____
_____
_____
_____
_____
_____
_____
_____
_____
_____
_____
_____
_____
_____
_____
_____
_____
_____

CHAPTER 7

THINKING OR FEELING CHILD

The **third Personality Type preference** we will look at relates to how your child/children form their decisions (their decision-making process):

Thinking (T) Thinking Type children seek *logical* reasons for making their decisions. They are usually rational and fair, seek honesty and look at consequences. They ask 'Why?'

Feeling (F) Feeling Type children refer to what is important to them – their *values* – to make their decisions. They enjoy harmonious relationships, consider the impact of their decisions on people and like to be appreciated. They ask 'Who?'

So, what is *your* child's decision-making process?

You may recall from earlier chapters that both Types, Thinker and Feeler, use their thoughts and feelings. This is about using logic/values for decision making. Remember, children can use both preferences, but one will feel more natural to them and is usually their first response to a situation.

> Please read both the Thinking/Feeling child sections before ticking the boxes. (For multiple children, perhaps use a different coloured pen for each child.)

THE THINKING (T) CHILD

Logic – Fairness – Problem solving

Stomp, stomp, slam, slam.
We all have conflict with our offspring, but resolving issues can be made simpler when we work with our knowledge of Types. I am a Feeling Type and my daughter, Cassie, is a Thinking Type. My initial response to an argument is to find a solution quickly and restore harmony and balance as soon as possible. However, Cassie's Thinking response is to spot flaws in my argument, and debate these flaws with critiquing logic. When she was younger, if no resolution was found, she would storm off to her bedroom and slam the door. Overwhelmed by the need for a positive outcome, I would follow her to her room. But instead of knocking respectfully, I would barge in and try to hug her, all the while pouring out apologies for upsetting her. As a Feeling Type, I thought this would mend our fences, but instead my actions were usually met by a hostile request for me to get out and leave her alone. Cassie would sit in stony silence as I reluctantly left the room.

My Thinking child and me

After repeated episodes of this unproductive behaviour, I realised that my way of dealing with her anger and frustration was not working. I was overwhelming her with my emotional need to be affirmed and create harmony, when what she needed was to regain emotional balance by being left alone to view the situation clearly. I finally asked her what I should do. Cassie told me she detested how emotional and clingy I was, because it made her feel angrier.

Cassie's blatant honesty challenged the way I managed conflict. I need to regain a harmonious equilibrium as soon as possible, but Cassie does not! I learned from this conversation not to overwhelm her with my feelings, but instead give her time to defuse and gather her emotions together. When I changed my behaviour, Cassie changed hers. She became calmer, more forgiving and more understanding of my emotional behaviour – although this varies depending on the topic! By understanding our differences in how we resolve conflict, Cassie and I have deepened our trust in each other and have improved the way we solve our disputes.

What have you noticed about your child?

Do they enjoy engaging in logical, critiquing conversation?

Tick the boxes that you think best describe your child/children's preferences

Thinking Children often:

- Ask 'Why?' and need a logical answer
- Say what they are thinking, with no 'filter' about the effect that it might have on other people's feelings
- Can upset people for the reason above, but do not do so deliberately. In their eyes they are merely telling the truth
- Like to figure things out. If they are Extraverted they will do this out loud, while an Introvert will usually figure things out in their head
- Make choices based on what makes sense and appears to be the most logical option
- Like to solve problems
- Work hard to be the best
- Will look at what is wrong first before noticing what is right. They often need to have this pointed out to them, as they forget about the positive things in life
- Feel it is not necessary to comment on the positives, as these are obvious. Would rather spend time on improvements and have a 'How can we improve?' mindset
- Expect competence in themselves and others. They will not respect people who are incompetent
- Enjoy making decisions independently
- Look for the emotion behind a decision *after* seeing the logic

THE FEELING (F) CHILD

Values - Harmony – Empathy

The right words at the right time.
Emotionally, Thinking and Feeling Types can be very different in the way they solve difficult family situations. Emily is a Feeling Type child, who is caring and empathetic with everyone she meets. She is always sensitive and considerate of other people's feelings, and it makes her happy to know that she can help others. Her friends love her and often turn to her in times of unhappiness or stress. Her father, Andrew, is a Thinking Type who verbalises, often without filter, whatever is on his mind. He is well known for putting people off side with his blunt, logical, critiquing language.

When Emily was young, she and her father were on a very turbulent flight together. Emily was distraught and fearful that the plane might crash – however unlikely that might actually be. When Andrew saw her fear, he simply blurted out the first words that came into his head. 'Don't worry,' he said, 'We won't crash today. Crashes usually happen on take-off or landing, or due to acts of terrorism.' He thought this straightforward presentation of clear facts would calm his daughter. Then he joked, or at least thought he joked, 'Anyway, if we go down, the good part is we go down together.' As you can imagine, this 'information' and the subsequent 'joke' did nothing to stop Emily sobbing.

Was Emily's father uncaring? No, of course not. From his perspective, he had given his daughter a logical, factual and direct response – one that he, as a Thinking Type, would have found comforting under similar circumstances. But Emily was unable to understand why her father could not comfort her with compassion and warmth. As a Feeling Type, what Emily needed was a demonstration of her father's empathy, and reassurance presented in a sensitive way. She needed to have her fears dispelled with words like, 'It's okay, turbulence happens all the time and it won't make the plane crash. I am here for you. Hold my hand and we will get through this together!'

The power of understanding the other preference is immeasurable when communicating with someone of the opposite Type. It's a mistake to assume others are thinking the way you do. 'Walking a mile in their shoes', and learning to express yourself in a way that resonates with them, will help people of the opposite Type feel understood and appreciated. It's gold in the relationship bank. Feeling Type children will benefit from understanding and learning about the personality differences between them and Thinking Types. This will give the Feeler the chance to change their reaction to language that they potentially might find hurtful.

What have you noticed about your child?

Do they like to be appreciated for their kindness and empathy?

THINKING OR FEELING CHILD

Tick the boxes that you think best describe your child/children's preferences

Feeling children often:

- ○ Are sensitive to the needs and feelings of others and will try not to say hurtful things to them
- ○ Like to help others
- ○ Make decisions based on their values
- ○ Strive for harmony in their relationships and the relationships of those around them. Disharmony is stressful for them
- ○ Enjoy positive feedback and like to be accepted
- ○ See the positive in a situation before the negative
- ○ Trust that others will reciprocate the way that they feel
- ○ Misinterpret, and therefore feel hurt by, the Thinker's direct, straightforward language
- ○ Want to be loved by most people
- ○ Value being able to help others and keep the balance of harmony and happiness at any cost
- ○ Feel hurt and upset when the Thinker's logical decision-making processes fail to preserve harmony and accord
- ○ Are more affected emotionally by events

WHO IS THIS MONSTER (OR TREASURE) IN MY HOUSE?

Refer back to the statements that you ticked and decide which Type best describes your child/ children.

(I have provided options for three children. You may need to write your own for additional children.)

Tick the most suitable box:

- ◯ My child is Feeling (F)
- ◯ My child is Thinking (T)
- ◯ I am unsure
- ◯ My child is Feeling (F)
- ◯ My child is Thinking (T)
- ◯ I am unsure
- ◯ My child is Feeling (F)
- ◯ My child is Thinking (T)
- ◯ I am unsure

MBTI: F = Feeling and T = Thinking

THINKING OR FEELING CHILD

Moments when you realise that there are no monsters – just buried treasures waiting to be found.

Summarise your thoughts

CHAPTER 8

JUDGING OR PERCEIVING CHILD

The **fourth Personality Type preference** that we will be looking at relates to how your child/children live their *outer life* (their lifestyle):

Judging (J) Judging Type children prefer their outer life to be planned and structured. They usually seek closure.

Perceiving (P) Perceiving Type children prefer an outer life that is flexible. They enjoy exploring options that give them room for spontaneity in their daily lives.

What is your child's lifestyle preference?

Do they naturally conform to routines and find this comforting, or are they more unpredictable and scattered?

Remember, children use both preferences, but one will feel more comfortable and is usually their first, more natural response to a situation.

> Please read both the Judging/ Perceiving child sections before ticking the boxes. (For multiple children, perhaps use a different coloured pen for each child.)

THE PERCEIVING (P) CHILD

Flexible – Adaptable – Spontaneous

Last-minute dash.
Cassie's friend, James, is a Perceiving Type. Like most Perceiving Types, he enjoys a flexible, spontaneous lifestyle. He is able to adapt and change as new experiences, ideas and situations come into his life. Work and play are both important to him, but highly structured schedules and diaries are not his thing. I remember the day I was listening to James talk to Cassie, discussing an assignment that he had just realised was due at midnight. He vaguely remembered it being given out several weeks before, but did not make note of the deadline as it seemed so far away. Suddenly inspired by the looming deadline, as Perceivers often are, James immediately sat down and started working feverishly for the few hours he had left to complete the assignment.

Perceiving Types focus better when the due date of an assignment is closer, but midnight was a little too close even for James! It was 11pm when he realised that he had actually let this project slide for a little too long, and he wasn't going to be able to finish it before midnight. Turning his computer off, James rationalised to us that he would lose ten per cent of his mark for not completing the work on time, but gain twenty per cent if he handed in a better assignment – and an extra twenty-four hours would allow him to do that. Cassie and I are both Perceivers and totally understand the last-minute dash, but even we were blown away by his relaxed logic. We did agree, however, that his plan made sense. James followed through with his plan and, as he predicted, managed to get a respectable mark – in fact a distinction – for his assignment.

This young man has always gained credits and distinctions for his work. His Judging Type parents live in constant stress, alarmed by the precipitous way he approaches life. But Perceivers control their world by being flexible and adaptable, and enjoy keeping their options open until the last moment. As James says, 'If I was failing I would change, but I'm not, so it's all good.'

If the work has great value to them, the Perceiving child will pull out all stops and strive to achieve their best results. If not, they are happy to meander through life, often succeeding in a 'just made it' manner, much to Judging Types' disbelief!

What have you noticed about your child?

Do they love the last-minute dash?

Tick the boxes that you think best describe your child/children's preferences

Perceiving children often:

- ○ Adapt easily to change and are flexible in their expectations of themselves and others
- ○ Like to play first and work later, or at least have some 'play' while working
- ○ Like to be able to explore any kind of idea or activity, and enjoy surprises as these provide them with more options and ideas
- ○ Find it difficult to start their work too soon; if they do they may feel as though they're not doing their best
- ○ Find it easier to focus on activities when close to the deadline, whether it's assignments, tasks or chores
- ○ Enjoy starting many projects at once and feel comfortable doing this
- ○ Are happy rushing to complete tasks at the last minute because they do not value perfection
- ○ Can be overwhelmed if all of the half-finished jobs have the same deadline. However, their adrenaline kicks in and often they have their best ideas at the last minute and get the job done
- ○ Like to keep their options open until the last minute
- ○ Are in control of their world by being flexible and able to adapt
- ○ Find activities can be boring if there are not enough choices
- ○ Find that tidiness and structure are not always their strengths. However, it is worth encouraging them to be tidy and better organised by making the associated activities fun and interesting

THE JUDGING (J) CHILD

Planned – Structured – Organised

The planning police.
From a very early age, as I tucked my son, Jack, into bed, he would ask me, 'What are we doing tomorrow?' I am a Perceiving parent and usually have no idea. I don't normally plan my day that far ahead. I would tell him whatever I thought he might want to hear. After our chat he would happily snuggle down into his bed, and I would wander off with little thought about the repercussions of my words.

The following day we would be out and about, doing a variety of things and altering the schedule according to my whims. When we arrived home, Jack would often be out of sorts. When I questioned him, his answer would be, 'We didn't do anything you said we would do today.' 'Oh, my goodness,' I would reply, 'I didn't know there was a planning policeman in my house!'

This occurred many times before I realised that my unscheduled actions greatly affected how Jack coped with his day. He liked to look forward to planned activities, and felt cheated when they didn't happen. When the schedule he had in his head didn't materialise, he would feel unsettled, stressed and insecure. I could see that I needed to change my behaviour. I discussed our personality differences with him, and explained that we would make firm plans for some activities the following day, but leave some time for spontaneity. I told him I would try to give him warning in advance when changes happened, but also tried to help him understand that some things in life happen unexpectedly.

The result of these discussions and changes in my behaviour was a happier, calmer child and a more organised parent. We both learned that our least preferred behaviour could develop and grow with practise and time.

What have you noticed about your child?

Do they like to know the schedule of what is happening in their day/week?

Tick the boxes that you think best describe your child/children's preferences

Judging Children often:

- ○ Like to be given a plan. They want to know what is going to happen
- ○ Respond well to structure
- ○ Like clear rules and procedures
- ○ Can be very stressed by a change of plans
- ○ Make decisions as soon as they believe they have the required facts. This can be to their detriment, as sometimes important information that appears later cannot be used
- ○ Are great at planning and organising
- ○ Can be great organisers, but can also become 'bossy' if this skill is not guided in the right direction
- ○ Do their work before their 'play'
- ○ See plans and promises as locked-in commitments
- ○ Start projects well before the deadline and usually complete them ahead of or on time
- ○ Write lists, whether in their heads or on paper
- ○ Can find it difficult to adapt or show flexibility

Refer back to the statements that you ticked and decide which Type best describes your child/ children.

(I have provided options for three children. You may need to write your own for additional children.)

Tick the most suitable box:

- ○ My child is Perceiving (P)
- ○ My child is Judging (J)
- ○ I am unsure

- ○ My child is Perceiving (P)
- ○ My child is Judging (J)
- ○ I am unsure

- ○ My child is Perceiving (P)
- ○ My child is Judging (J)
- ○ I am unsure

MBTI: P = Perceiving and J = Judging

WHO IS THIS MONSTER (OR TREASURE) IN MY HOUSE?

Moments when you realise that there are no monsters – just buried treasures waiting to be found.

Summarise your thoughts

PART 2

ACTION: SUMMARISE YOUR CHILD'S PERSONALITY TYPE

Now go back to the tick box at the end of each chapter in Part 2, and list below the letters that you chose from each of the four pairs of personality preferences. You can find the results for each child's Type on the following pages:

E/I: page 68
S/N: page 77
T/F: page 86
J/P: page 95

This will give you the Personality Type for your child/children. In other words, one letter from each pair of personality preferences is required to arrive at a four-letter Personality Type for each child. For example, *ESTJ, ENTP, ISFJ, INFP*.

Personality Type Child 1 :

Personality Type Child 2:

Personality Type Child 3:

Personality Type Child 4:

ISTJ	ISFJ	INFJ	INTJ
ISTP	ISFP	INFP	INTP
ESTP	ESFP	ENFP	ENTP
ESTJ	ESFJ	ENFJ	ENTJ

Don't be concerned if you ticked 'Unsure' for one (or all) of the four personality preferences discussed in chapters five to eight. As mentioned at the beginning of Part 2, children will begin to develop their Type during their early years. However, some children's personalities don't become more defined until their late teens. So, it's possible that your child's full preference may not be evident yet.

As your skills in utilising your knowledge about personalities and Type develop, you will recognise the different preferences when they appear and be able to respond with more understanding. Your child will be their most relaxed self and happiest when they are operating from their natural Type.

My ISTJ son and I continue to have a great relationship and he is now in his twenties

PART 3

FINDING THE 'GOLD' IN YOUR RELATIONSHIPS WITH YOUR CHILD/CHILDREN

By now you should have a pretty good idea of what Personality Type you are, what Type your partner is, and what Type your children are, or are becoming. I hope that, as you've read through the stories and anecdotes, you are beginning to feel confident that you can understand and recognise each Type. But that's only half the reason you're here. Simply understanding somebody doesn't guarantee a happy and harmonious relationship. You need to work with your understanding of Personality Types in a practical way in the real world, and that's what Part 3 is about.

The following chapters provide a brief overview of how different Personality Types can interact with each other in parent/child relationships. I hope that the tables and trouble-shooter tips will give you some ideas of how to understand your offspring and continue to develop long-lasting, loving relationships with them.

Each parent-child Personality Type combination is explored with personal anecdotes and easy-to-read tables that illustrate the troubles and treasures you're likely to encounter with each Type. I've also provided tools and tips to help you understand and manage your monsters/treasures.

Ready?

CHAPTER 9

EXTRAVERT – INTROVERT PARENT/CHILD RELATIONSHIPS

Let's start with the first letters of our profile: **Extravert (E) – Introvert (I) parent-child relationships**.

The **first Personality Type preference** relates to where you both get your energy from:

INTROVERT (I) PARENT WITH EXTRAVERT (E) CHILD

Energised by the inner world / Energised by the outer world

Silence is golden for some.
My brother picks me up from the airport, and from the back seat his Extravert daughter talks from the minute I get in. She asks questions, tells me about what is happening in her life, and interrupts any conversation my brother and I begin. After a few minutes of this, my Introvert brother says, 'Millie, can you just be quiet for five minutes?' Silence from the back

seat. I am a little concerned that her feelings have been hurt. No, thirty seconds later, she's back with a vengeance, talking without taking a breath. I smile; this is me when I was young (maybe even now).

Talking and the need for many friends is not only energising for the Extravert, it is part of their process for solving problems or exploring ideas they might have. By all means, encourage quiet times when they are left in their own company, but please do not shut them down for too long. If you do this too often, it can cause learning difficulties and mental health issues. Let your Extraverts 'get it out of their system' – the need to talk is part of their DNA. Remember that talking and socialising can be their treasures; they can get a conversation rolling and make people feel comfortable. But this tendency can also be one of their monsters. When their constant conversation becomes overpowering, this is the time to encourage reflective listening or even silence.

Table 1: Treasures and troubles of the I parent and the E child

TREASURES	TROUBLES
I parents are good listeners.	I parents can be exhausted and annoyed by the E child's need for social stimulation and constant chatter.
I parents can teach the E child that 'silence can be golden'.	I parents may shut down/be dismissive of the E child while the child talks through their thoughts.
I parents can help the E child by making thoughtful decisions for them and limiting choices that could otherwise become overwhelming. For example, having too many friends/commitments, experiencing constant changes in their environment or having too many decisions to make.	I parents can fail to see/be dismissive of the E child's need to have a large number of friends, many Facebook friends and a wide variety of people in their lives, but having this busy social life energises the E child.
I parents can encourage the E child to think their thoughts through before acting on them.	I parents might stifle inspired, spur-of-the-moment thoughts that may energise the E child.
I parents can help the E child focus on collecting their thoughts before speaking.	I parents may not encourage social group interaction/collaboration or speaking in public.
I parents can encourage quieter one-on-one activities or those involving private reflection and introspection for the E child.	I parents can have difficulty understanding that constant interaction/activity stimulates and energises their E child.
I parents provide a quiet place to 'land' when down time is required.	I parents can be perceived by the E child as boring, distant and unresponsive, causing the E child to look to other people for social stimulation.

Treasure Tools and Tips for the Introvert parent to use with their Extravert child

1. Many Introverted parents cannot believe the amount of words that come out of their Extravert child's mouth. Do listen and acknowledge your Extravert child's statements. Among the overflow of words, there are important matters to discuss.
2. The Introvert parent often feels the need to shut down the Extravert child's chatter. Avoid doing this, as talking helps your child's thought processes and creative energy.
3. Extraverts talk, think, then talk again. Help your child stay on track by selecting from their conversation the key matter under consideration and then gently bring them back to that topic.
4. Introverted parents can teach the Extraverted child valuable lessons about listening 'to hear' others. Learning this skill will give your child downtime to collect their thoughts and focus their energies. This, of course, needs to be done in a fun and interesting way or concentration will be lost.
5. Don't assume that the Extravert child will need time alone. The company of others energises them! You may find your house overrun with your child's friends. Negotiate with them and allow them to choose two or three of their favourite playmates to have over. Doing so will help teach them to make good friendship choices.
6. The Introverted parent might be stressed at the 'superficial' thoughts of the Extraverted child. Extraverted children do not spend as much time on internal thoughts as their parents do. Creating a time and space for the Extraverted child to participate in a quiet but interesting activity, such as reading, knitting, puzzles or cards, can provide them with downtime and focus that will help them learn to reflect more deeply and develop the skill of introspection.
7. The study style of the Extravert is different from that of the Introvert. Engage your Extraverted child in discussion about their set homework. Talking about their homework helps their brain absorb and understand the concepts that they need to learn.

8. The older Extravert child might enjoy having friends to study with. This allows them to talk with others about their ideas and stimulates their thought processes. However, as Extraverts are easily distracted, having a goal to achieve by the end of their group study session will help keep them focused.
9. The Extravert child is often energetic and outgoing. If they are showing behaviours that are more Introverted than usual, see this as a stress indicator. It is important to follow this up with further discussion.

WHO IS THIS MONSTER (OR TREASURE) IN MY HOUSE?

Golden nuggets of wisdom found

Summarise your thoughts

INTROVERT (I) PARENT WITH INTROVERT (I) CHILD

Energised by the inner world / Energised by the inner world

Living in an Extraverted world.
Heather talks of her experience as an Introverted parent of Introverted children:

'My highest priority was the constant and consistent subjecting of my children to the "Extraverted world" in which we live. From birth I took the children everywhere – banks, shops, appointments, et cetera. All four children were taught to stand quietly in queues with hands at their sides and not touch anything or misbehave in any way. It wasn't a constant telling off (though certainly sometimes) but rather a quiet daily habit.

'When the children started to talk, they were expected to look at people and acknowledge them if they were spoken to. Every day, the children would meet and greet heaps of people, from the butcher to the baker to the candlestick maker!

'I also taught them to answer the phone and door safely and respectfully. I knew my children were like me (except Alex, my only Extraverted child), so I persevered and to this day I am glad I did, as they all talk on the phone well, answer politely, and address people with warmth and respect. As Introverts, I know they are out of their comfort zone, but I knew as their mother it was my duty to prepare them socially to engage with others.

'Interestingly, many parents thought I was tough on them because they were not allowed to play at the bank or shops, but if they had done so they may have been reprimanded by a stranger and I believe that would have crushed them. My core belief is that I wanted them armed and ready to cope with an Extraverted world. I should say that every one of us would breathe a huge sigh of relief when we arrived home, even the babies. Home certainly was our safe zone and remains so now.'

Table 2: treasures and troubles of the I parent and the I child

TREASURES	TROUBLES
I parent and I child have similar needs regarding how they are energised and choose to communicate. This creates harmony between them.	The I parent may not prepare the I child for the outer world.
I parent and I child respect and understand each other's need for re-grouping and quiet time.	It might not occur to the I parent to encourage group communication skills in their I child. For example, making eye contact, and voicing ideas and thoughts in front of others.
Both I parent and I child will enjoy quiet, reflective and focused conversation.	Important matters and feelings are not always openly discussed. This can lead to arguments/problems and the I child feeling that no-one understands them.
Neither I parent nor I child need to have many people around them.	The I parent might not encourage multiple friendships/activities/interests and having friends over to stay.
Non-verbal communication methods will be welcomed by both I parent and I child. Leaving notes, texting, Facebook posts and other online discussion forums are completely acceptable and comfortable for both.	Communication with the outer world involves verbal interactions and I children need to develop skills in this area to make themselves heard. Introverts have much to offer but can be overlooked in the E world.
Both I parent and I child undertake careful internal consideration of ideas before making a verbal response. They will patiently wait in silence for the other to speak.	The I parent may find it difficult to talk when embarrassed, upset or angry, but externalising these emotions may be valuable to the I child, as it teaches them how to express their own emotions. Expressing emotions is essential so that others don't have to 'mind read' to understand the I child's emotional needs.
Sharing deeply considered ideas and plans makes it easier to move forward with decisions on mutual ground.	Externalising thoughts and ideas can be stressful for both I parent and I child.

Treasure Tools and Tips for the Introvert parent to use with their Introvert child

1. In the Extraverted world, Introverts are constantly working against their preferred Type. It is important for the Introverted parent to help build their child's social skills, such as holding their own space in conversations, using eye contact, and verbalising their feelings and emotions.
2. If the Introverted parent can help the Introverted child build proficiency in social skills, the I child will have a less awkward, more natural response to the external world and will appear and feel more confident.
3. The Introverted child and parent can live in great harmony, with neither imposing on the other's space or privacy. Conversation is often kept to the minimum and is non- confrontational. However, real life is full of confrontational conversations, so ensure that you are both prepared for this.
4. The Introverted parent does not always see the necessity for their child to have friends visit or even to have their own friends over. This can mean a relaxed and stress-free environment, but once again it is important to push the boundaries to help the Introverted child socialise with other people.
5. Often, troublesome issues are not discussed or aired until they have been internally 'stewing' for too long. This lack of open conversation and mutual understanding can lead to an uncomfortable 'blow up', which is often exaggerated in its intensity. Feelings do need to be discussed and explored verbally, not just through the Introvert's preferred, written communication methods such as text or email.
6. Introverts usually listen more than talk, and can often be overwhelmed by rapid, loud conversation. Teach your child how to have answers to the onslaught of questions that people will throw at them. If appropriate, they can use phrases such as, 'Let me think on that and I will give you an answer tomorrow.' Or, 'I can give you a quick answer on the spot, but if you would like to hear

my considered thoughts can you give me a few minutes?' Asking people for time is important, as others are often not aware of the time it takes for Introverts to form a valuable answer.
7. Introverted children often don't like to be the centre of attention. Teach them to tolerate more attention than they are comfortable with by allowing them to dress up and role play.
8. Introverted children like time to think, but this is not always possible in the Extraverted world. Help them to make quick decisions when necessary – they won't always have time to reflect.
9. Encourage Introverted children to be flexible in their approach to tasks – they won't always be able to follow their preferred procedures.

EXTRAVERT (E) PARENT WITH INTROVERT (I) CHILD

Energised by the outer world / Energised by the inner world

Just be with me.
When my son, Jack, was four years old, we had a memorable day at the supermarket together. As we walked up and down the aisles, I bumped into two different friends, had a conversation with each of them, and organised two future coffee dates. Then I saw a woman looking lost and offered to help her. Next I directed that person to the correct aisle for the item she needed. I helped a little old lady get a can of soup from a high shelf. Jack patiently sat in the trolley in silence, observing my social and emotional behaviour. I was on fire! So many new and old friends. I was chatting to the shop assistant at the checkout when he reached over and held my face in his two little hands. He looked me in the eyes and said, 'Mummy, can you not talk to anyone else?' Oh, the life of the Introverted son with the Extraverted mother! But I was lucky to have a son who not only understood what was happening, but could verbalise his feelings – something that, as an Extravert, I was able to model for him. I understood at once that he needed some downtime with me. 'Certainly,' I said, and we went and sat down together and ate our ice-creams, just the two of us. He was happy. I was all his.

Table 3: treasures and troubles of the E parent and the I child

TREASURES	TROUBLES
An E parent's constant exposure of their I child to people can help the child build stronger social skills and feel greater ease in social situations.	E parents can exhaust the I child with too much talk and socialising.
E parents can bring a different, more energising dynamic to the I child's life. This helps them learn to act more quickly in response to answering questions or taking action in the Extraverted world.	E parents are often impulsive and do not give the I child time to reflect when answering questions or choosing actions.
E parents can help their I child become comfortable interacting with the Extraverted world by talking them through situations and encouraging confident conversations.	E parents often wrongly assume that their I child is shy, when in fact they are quietly confident. The parent may focus on 'curing' the shyness instead of simply encouraging them to communicate and interact more freely with the external world of people.
E parents often have a fun and stimulating environment in their homes.	E parents do not give the I child time to 'chill out' and re-energise.
E parents can negotiate pathways in friendships and schooling that might be too stressful for the I child to navigate alone.	E parents can be seen as bossy and interfering.
E parents can often 'dig' into the I child's reserve by persistent questioning; they can find out what is happening for them emotionally and help resolve problems through verbal discussion.	If poorly handled, the E parent's 'digging' can invade the I child's personal space and thoughts. The I child may not give true answers if threatened by what they perceive to be personally invasive questions.
E parents can share any concerns the I child may have with others in order to get changes or results on their behalf.	E parents may share details of conversations with their I child with others, often without confirming whether their child wants those details shared. This can destroy the I child's trust, and once 'burnt' they will not share again.

**Treasure Tools and Tips for the Extravert
parent to use with their Introvert child**

1. Introverts like to think-talk-think. As an Extraverted parent, it is important for you to give time for your Introverted child to answer any questions or ideas that you might 'throw' at them. It is valuable to give them a time frame in which to answer. For example, 'Have a think about that and I'll get back to you in half an hour.'
2. Constant verbal chatter and overstimulation can exhaust the Introverted child. The mindful Extravert parent will give the Introverted child time to 'chill out'.
3. The Introverted child is not unfriendly or necessarily shy. There is nothing wrong with them; they simply do not require constant stimulation. Let them be!
4. Extraverted parents like to encourage their children to have friends and will invite people over to play with them and entertain them. Don't invite friends around without their permission.
5. Introverted children are often happy to be by themselves or in the company of one or maybe two other children; any more can be overpowering. This is okay. Do not bring in the troops.
6. The Extraverted parent is great for 'stretching' the Introvert's opposite preference. This is important, as Introverts need to be able to function socially and emotionally in an Extraverted world. Just don't overdo it for your own benefit.
7. *Teaching* Introvert children the skills to communicate and function in their own style and at their own pace is a gift that the Extravert parent can give their child. *Forcing* them to do so in an Extraverted fashion is not! It is overwhelming for them.
8. Understanding that Introverted children feel more comfortable revealing their emotions and feelings through written language is valuable knowledge for the Extraverted parent. Texts, cards and letters can be a great form of communication for parent and child.
9. Extraverts can be impulsive decision makers, whereas Introverted children may need time to consider potential actions before committing to them. This can be frustrating for both parties, as each is stressed – either by the other's excessive speed or their lack of it. The Extraverted adult's maturity and knowledge can be used to ease the way for both parties.

WHO IS THIS MONSTER (OR TREASURE) IN MY HOUSE?

Golden nuggets of wisdom found

Summarise your thoughts

EXTRAVERT (E) PARENT WITH EXTRAVERT (E) CHILD

Energised by the outer world / Energised by the outer world

Let's talk it through.
My daughter, Cassie, and I are both Extraverts. We need to talk to think. When Cassie was younger, she would sit with me at the kitchen breakfast bar to do her homework. She found it beneficial and energising to talk about her homework. She was able to solve problems out loud and talk through the topic being studied. Both Extraverts, we liked to intersperse study conversation with myriad other topics – initially friends and toys, then later clothes and boys. If we were off the homework topic for too long, I would steer us back to the study front. We both knew that if we kept referring back to her schoolwork, progress would be made, and we would both have fun. Learning was easier for her when she was able to talk the subject through, and it also meant that I got to hear about her school day and any important incidents, good or bad, that may have happened along the way. Helping unpack her mind this way created the room she needed to be able to concentrate on schoolwork. Try this some time with your Extraverted child, but ensure that you both keep coming back to the key topic at hand.

Table 4: treasures and troubles of the E parent and the E child

TREASURES	TROUBLES
Both E parent and E child enjoy a busy social schedule and have lots of fun together.	The E parent and E child can make others feel isolated when in their company, and can become overly involved in each other's lives.
Both E parent and E child enjoy being able to converse freely together to 'think' things through.	The E parent may not teach their E child how to learn to listen to others.
The E parent and E child have open lines of communication.	Both E parent and E child can engage in talking without thinking, and without damage control.
Both E parent and E child tend to enjoy being the centre of attention and can be very entertaining.	Both E parent and E child can be attention-seeking. Not everybody wants to applaud you.
The E parent understands how to keep the E child motivated and on task by talking things through.	When serious work is required, the two Es can get distracted and go off topic for too long.
Both E parent and E child enjoy participating in many different friendship groups and often have many people they regard as friends.	The E parent and E child can appear to others to be superficial in their friendships, as other people may enjoy a greater 'intensity' than the Extravert is able to give.
The two Es enjoy listening to conversations and being a part of them.	The E parent needs to teach the E child about confidentiality, as they will often relay to others what they have heard without thinking about the consequences.

Treasure Tools and Tips for the Extravert parent to use with their Extravert child

1. The combination of two Extraverts can lead to an exciting and busy social schedule. When it becomes overloaded it can be stressful, even for Extraverts. Be astute and learn to recognise how much is too much for you both.
2. This people-loving duo can leave other members of their families (particularly the Introverts) feeling left out or invaded, as they fulfil their need for socialising by either going out with friends or inviting them home. Thinking about different family members' feelings and needs should always be considered and discussed with all concerned.
3. Teach your Extraverted child, by demonstrating through your own actions, to actively listen and 'hear' others rather than blithely talk over the top of them in conversations. This will give your child an important life skill. *(See the appendix on page 187 for a definition of Active listening.)*
4. The combination of two Extraverts means that conversations can be diverse and fast, with the subject matter changing constantly. Usually you will both understand the matters being discussed, but be aware that it is all a muddle of words to an outsider.
5. Do not become overinvolved in your Extraverted child's social life, even though you will hear so much about it.
6. Discuss the importance of thinking before speaking and give examples of 'foot in mouth' mistakes that you may have made. This will help your young Extravert understand that their natural tendency to speak their thoughts immediately can be damaging to others and themselves.
7. If the lines of communication and understanding about themselves are open, the Extraverted parent and Extraverted child can have a lot of fun together in the external world. So, keep talking, broach a broad range of topics, ask questions and look interested. The Extraverted child usually likes being the centre of attention, and will respond well to this.

8. Study and learning for the Extraverted child needs to include conversation and talking out loud, as that is how the Extravert's brain understands the concepts being taught. Teach your child how to stay on task, as many topics besides the work itself will be discussed.
9. Encourage your child to recognise the diversity of their friendships and how to nurture these individually.

CHAPTER 10

SENSING – INTUITION PARENT/CHILD RELATIONSHIPS

Now let's look at **Sensing (S) – Intuition (N) parent-child relationships**. This personality preference is about the way you and your child take in information:

INTUITIVE (N) PARENT WITH SENSING (S) CHILD

Big picture versus details

Can we see the world and not stay at home?

My Intuitive friend, Greg, has two Sensing sons. They are homebodies who love their routines of work, gaming and quiet catch-ups with friends on weekends. They rarely vary the details of daily life, do not seek change or travel, and are content with their lives. They are interested in facts that they know and the practical reality of situations, where life follows an orderly, sequential pattern.

As their parent, Greg is frustrated by this. He would love them to experience the world beyond their secure routines and find new, challenging things to do. He wants his sons to be inspired by the things in life that he sees as important and exciting. He is mindful of different Personality Types, but likes to throw them as many 'curveballs' as he can. He takes them to restaurants so that they can experience different cuisines from places like Asia and Africa, even though he knows they prefer their tried and true schnitzels and steak. He also takes them camping, even though it stresses them out somewhat. He knows that stretching their experience will be good for them.

Greg pushes and prods his sons' safe world with ideas about finding jobs overseas, travelling to countries like Brazil where life is 'precarious but interesting' and would provide a great learning experience for them. Greg has even gone to the extremes of bribery, such as taking his boys to see their favourite band in New York City, just to get them outside their world and into his. Expensive, but successful! A good time was had by all, but Greg's sons were pleased to get home to their comfort zone.

As an Intuitive parent, Greg will continue to gently push his sons outside their comfort zone so that he can stretch their boundaries and ideas. But he also knows that his sons are happy with the immediate, realistic focus of their lives. He acknowledges that their desires and his are like 'chalk and cheese', and their requirements for happiness are being fulfilled differently.

Table 5: treasures and troubles of the N parent and the S child

TREASURES	TROUBLES
The N parent can help the S child to investigate and understand new ideas.	The N parent could introduce ideas that are beyond the S child's 'reach'.
The N parent can show the S child new and different ways of doing things.	The S child's reluctance to accept change or alter routines can be frustrating and annoying for the N parent.
The N parent will be able to give the S child experiences that they never dreamed of.	While constantly looking to future possibilities, the N parent may not allow the S child to live in the moment.
The N parent can create change in the S child's life and prevent things from sometimes becoming boring.	The N parent can overwhelm the S child with too much change.
The N parent can teach the S child to question what is going on in the world and how it affects them, and show them new possibilities.	Constant questioning, and wanting the child to be aware of changes, can be very disturbing for the S child, who is often happiest just being.
The N parent enjoys the discovery of new ideas and learning opportunities, and can see the big picture/future implications from the outset.	The S child requires some repetition and consistency in their world in order to build up to the big picture. They may become stressed and confused without the 'building blocks'.
The N parent looks for a more stimulating and diverse approach to educating their child in both life and school. The S child benefits from the 'stretch' that this provides as they mature.	The N parent finds it stressful when they have to present ideas to their S offspring in the detailed, ordered way that their child feels comfortable with.

Treasure Tools and Tips for the Intuitive parent to use with their Sensing child

1. Practise experiencing the world as your child does – with your senses. Give your child more detailed explanations and concrete experiences.
2. Sensing children require sequential steps and detail when receiving instructions; use this knowledge in your communication.
3. Be aware that your idea of an 'exciting adventure' could be too much for the Sensing child. Check in with how they feel so that you don't overwhelm them. Connect new ideas to current realities in their lives so that they can link them to their known facts.
4. The Intuitive parent's viewpoints are very valuable to the Sensing child, as they can help their children explore and understand new ideas and theories. But this process needs to be started from the bottom of the stairs, so to speak. Step your child to the top of the stairs and they will be able to enjoy these novel experiences.
5. Intuitive parents may become frustrated or annoyed with their Sensing child's need for details and apparent lack of desire for change. Understand that your Sensing child's need for repetition and routine is not boring or unimaginative; these are the best ways for them to learn. Allow them to follow this process, but stretch them and add some bigger-picture strategies, like brainstorming possible solutions to problems.
6. The Intuitive parent enjoys questioning and hypothesising about different scenarios and events, and feels that they can improve and change the world. You may think that it is important for your child to question their observations about the world around them, but a Sensing child may not want to do this. They are happy just being in the world, so don't always push your point of view. Let them be.
7. The Intuitive parent also worries about how their Sensing child will fit into the world of the future. Their concerns can cloud the joy of living in the moment. Make sure that these concerns do not overwhelm you.

SENSING – INTUITION PARENT/CHILD RELATIONSHIPS

8. The Intuitive parent may become frustrated and bored with their Sensing child, who is happy to live in the here and now. You are the adult and you now have the knowledge about personalities, so enjoy today with your child!
9. Bring your new plans or theories down to earth when presenting them to your Sensing child. Give them information on specific realities, details and immediate applications of these. Then guide them gently towards your ideas, which for them may seem to be coming from another planet.

WHO IS THIS MONSTER (OR TREASURE) IN MY HOUSE?

Golden nuggets of wisdom found

Summarise your thoughts

SENSING (S) PARENT WITH SENSING (S) CHILD

Details = details

Same same, not different.

My whole family are Sensing Types. This is very obvious when it comes to the kind of holidays we take and the activities we choose to do when we travel. As we are very sensory, where we stay is important to us, and we like the comfort of staying in familiar surroundings. So when we travel we choose hotels from the same chain, so that we see the same brand of coffee in the mini bar, the same colour sheets on the bed and the same uniforms on the staff. When we reach our destination, we visit the most popular and generic tourist sites. We usually find a restaurant that we like within the first couple of days, and this is where we go for most of our meals. It feels familiar and comforting. We also have favourite holiday destinations that we have visited several times, because we know they won't hold any surprises and we know all the details of how to get there and where to stay.

Trying something new and different, such as catching trains in a foreign city, is daunting for my Sensing family, but knowing that we have a familiar hotel room to come back to helps ground us so that we don't miss out on the broadening and stretching experiences that travel provides. We also sometimes holiday with friends who are Intuitives, who encourage us to step out of our comfort zones. One year our friend, Michael, took us by helicopter to a small deserted island for a picnic. It was an interesting experience, and I'm glad that we were up for it, but we still value our tried and true destinations and activities. They're the ones that are truly relaxing. Too many changes and different experiences compromise the enjoyment of our holidays. Give us measurable holidays that we have researched and hold few surprises, and we are happy little Vegemites.

Table 6: treasures and troubles of the S parent and the S child

TREASURES	TROUBLES
Both S parent and S child are in touch with their five senses and live in the comfort of the present together.	The S parent and S child can stay in the 'safety' of the known facts and details forever if not forced to make adjustments in life.
The S parent and S child often enjoy similar activities and stay within their comfort zone. This means that they live peacefully and in harmony.	The S parent is not always able to offer and encourage new ideas and experiences for either their S child or themselves.
They have similar learning styles, which makes it easier for the S parent to help the S child process and learn information.	Both S parent and S child might find it difficult to create new ideas or find ways of handling new projects.
Change is not always important. The S child is happy in the routines and details of daily life, and does not require constant stimulation to prevent them from becoming bored.	S parents might not think to encourage their S child to look at future possibilities.
The S parent and S child often share a pragmatic, 'sensible' outlook on life.	The S parent can be too 'sensible', and lack the desire for adventure and change that can help their child grow.
The S parent can provide a stable environment for their S child.	Living in the present does not prepare S children for the inevitable fluctuations that the future brings.
S parents keep everyday life constant. This makes both S parent and S child feel 'safe'.	This stability can make it hard to keep up with the necessary and constant changes that technological/environmental/political innovations bring.

Treasure Tools and Tips for the Sensing parent to use with their Sensing child

1. The Sensing parent and their Sensing child will enjoy using their five senses to experience the world and will often enjoy similar activities. 'Stretch' yourself and your child by seeking new experiences.
2. The Sensing parent will usually teach their child using details and facts. They start at the beginning of the learning process and use repetition and revision for reinforcement. Expand the Sensing child's learning style to include big-picture frameworks, such as new concepts and theories. You can do this in areas that the child is familiar with.
3. The Sensing parent lives life in the present. They might not have the vision to imagine the future. This will limit the Sensing child's view of the world. Encourage them (and yourself) to explore new and diverse possibilities.
4. Both Sensing parent and Sensing child appreciate the here and now, and their expectations are usually sensible and pragmatic. Challenge your Sensing child (and yourself) with questions that take you outside your comfort zone, such as, 'What else? What's new? How can we change this to be even better? What are the possibilities?' Write them down and make some changes.
5. It may be challenging for the Sensing child to think of original and creative ideas for their schoolwork, preferring to use information they already have. As the parent, you can work with them to stretch their imagination (yours as well). Brainstorming concepts or even using an Inituitive's ideas can stimulate the Sensing person's vision.
6. Teaching the Sensing child about how the Intuitive thinks will be valuable. It is important for their communication with and understanding of others to appreciate and acknowledge the significance of these differences.
7. Practise 're-inventing the wheel' with your child. Take a known 'wheel' or experience and look for other ways to change the current process. Brainstorm your ideas on paper and see if you can come

up with any improvement or possible benefits. As a starting point, you might look at the process of bedtime rituals and discuss any changes that could make it better for you and your child.
8. Discuss with your Sensing child the language of the Intuitive and how difficult it can be for them to relate to, as the Intuitive's conversation is often full of metaphors and stories rather than real-life facts. Help them to understand the actual meaning of the Intuitive's conversation without dismissing them as unrealistic, 'head in the clouds' and overimaginative. Teach them not to bore the Intuitive with too many details.
9. Teach your child to accept people who dress, talk and behave in unconventional, quirky ways. Explain that these people just choose to express themselves differently, and often more visually. Their points of view and choices in life are just as valuable as those of Sensing Types, and need to be equally respected and valued.

SENSING – INTUITION PARENT/CHILD RELATIONSHIPS

Golden nuggets of wisdom found

Summarise your thoughts

INTUITIVE (N) PARENT WITH INTUITIVE (N) CHILD

Big picture / big picture

Celebrating our children's achievements.

I was discussing with friends how we all displayed our children's artwork. I put mine on the fridge, left it for a week, then discreetly 'transferred' it to the recycling. One of my Intuitive friends had a very different way of showcasing her children's schoolwork and other achievements in life. She explained...

'We had two huge windows across our family area which I never curtained until all the children had completed primary school. Each child had a portion of one window and their artwork, scribbles, certificates and merits were plastered all over it. It remained there until they decided to take it down. It was important that they knew they were valued individuals and to acknowledge what they had achieved. It was probably not the best blockout, but was the best view. It also showcased the children's works for visitors and became a talking point. In doing this I was able to see my Intuitive children's different talents and skills, as well as that of my Sensing child, and work out how to encourage them appropriately.'

Not right or wrong – just different strokes for different folks!

Table 7: treasures and troubles of the N parent and the N child

TREASURES	TROUBLES
The N parent can be imaginative and fun, and create games and activities that will thrill the N child.	The N parent might not be able to help the N child understand the mainly Sensing world that we live in.
The N parent will often be unconventional in some areas and will encourage their N child's differences and individual ideas.	Learning in the traditional schooling system might not suit the N child, and the N parent might be unable to help with conforming to the details of the literal, Sensing world.
The N parent and N child both look at life from a 'big picture' angle. Sharing ideas can be exciting and stimulating.	The N parent and N child's big-picture ideas may never come to fruition without anyone to help them see the details.
The N parent will accept and be excited by their N child's vision and possible 'quirkiness', viewing it as a strength rather than a weakness.	The N parent might not be able to help the N child adapt to the 'normality' of society and these children may be/feel isolated from others.
The N parent will be able to see their N child's big-picture ideas and encourage them to move forward with those ideas in their schooling/businesses/passions.	The N parent may encourage ideas that will never work and therefore leave the child deflated/disappointed.
The N child will feel accepted by and comfortable with an N parent.	The N child can feel like an outsider in the Sensing world.
The thoughts of the N parent and child have no barriers and they seek to create, grasp and share new ideas. They are the designers of the future.	The N child and parent become bored with too many facts and details and may disregard the conversation of Sensing people.

Treasure Tools and Tips for the Intuitive parent to use with their Intuitive child

1. The Intuitive will be a fun and imaginative parent for the Intuitive child. They will often create games and activities out of simple materials or just by using ideas and imagination. Be careful not to completely take over the child's games and activities with your 'great' ideas.
2. The Intuitive parent will make life fun for their Intuitive child's friends and create games that no-one else has played. Your child will enjoy this creativity, but their Sensing playmates may prefer to stick to familiar games that they already know. If this happens, ask the Sensing children what games they like and add your exciting games later.
3. The Intuitive parent and child often enjoy unconventional activities, styles of clothing, foods and behaviour, which can cause them to stand out from the crowd. This can lead to the child being excluded from conventional social traditions because they don't conform. Safeguard your child and help them find a platform of both individualism and acceptance.
4. The differences mentioned in points two and three can create a struggle for the Intuitive child, who is often searching for new ideas and theories. They might find it hard to understand the 'limiting' thoughts of the Sensing Types. Explain that Sensing people like to start their ideas at the 'bottom of the stairs', and they will have to patiently explain all the small details of their exciting ideas if they want their Sensing friends to understand.
5. Teach the Intuitive child to understand the Sensing world they live in, early in life. It will give them the knowledge and information to make decisions about the way they want to integrate themselves and their ideas and values into society. This can prevent these children feeling isolated and different.
6. Intuitive parents and children have a positive view of the future. They can 'turn lemons into lemonade'. Without focusing too much on the detail, they see big-picture possibilities and have

different ways of solving problems. They are often inspirational conversationalists for those looking for solutions. Make sure you encourage this.
7. With encouragement from their Intuitive parents, Intuitive children can be changemakers of the future. Reinforcing the use of their gifts, while also teaching them how to interact with Sensing people, can help the Intuitive child 'sell' their ground-breaking idea to a Sensing world.
8. Both Intuitive parent and Intuitive child enjoy learning and creating lots of different things in different ways. They like to know the main idea but not the details, so may struggle when it comes to producing anything that they invent or design. If this becomes an issue, bring in a Sensing Type to help get the project off the ground and into the big-picture cloud.
9. The Intuitive parent may need to introduce some grounding discipline to key activities so that their Intuitive child can learn to rein in their free spirit when necessary.

WHO IS THIS MONSTER (OR TREASURE) IN MY HOUSE?

Golden nuggets of wisdom found

Summarise your thoughts

SENSING (S) PARENT WITH INTUITIVE (I) CHILD

Details versus big picture

We can all succeed.

Tom was an imaginative child who was always making up stories, creating costumes and inventing imaginary friends. By the age of twelve, Tom was 'king' of the kids in his street. His ability to create a world of fun and fantasy made him exciting and fun to be with. As he progressed through his teen years, he made friends with likeminded people, but their unique ideas and plans seemed wacky and strange to many others. His mother thought of Tom as quirky, and he was quite different from her other two children. She worried that he lived too much in a world of make-believe, and spent years trying to help him focus on the present and practical aspects of the world. She desperately tried to fill his life with details and routines. His mother was consumed with dread that he would never get a 'real' job. After all, who would want someone as strange as her son? But her fears were unfounded. Today Tom heads up a marketing company, using his imagination, vision and big-picture perspective to successfully market and sell to clients all over the world. He is using his Intuitive preference and living his dream – his mother's fears were unfounded.

How would you have felt if you were Tom's mother?

Table 8: treasures and troubles of the S parent and the N child

TREASURES	TROUBLES
The S parent can teach the N child how to handle the practicalities of life.	The S parent can think that their N child is quirky and strange, and be concerned that they do not fit their idea of the 'norm'.
The S parent can show their N child that it is the small details that are at the base of creative ideas and performance.	The S parent wants their N child to start at the beginning, with the details, which can stifle innovation.
The S parent can help their N child to attend to at least some of the necessary details to make sure that their big-picture ideas can come to fruition.	The S parent often struggles to understand the N child's big-picture outlook.
S parents can show the N child how to progress from the beginning to the end as an alternative to the N child's preferred starting point at the finish.	The S parent may be unable to engage in brainstorming and imaginative processes that 'feed' the N child's brain and creativity.
S parents are able to offer their N child a different outlook on life.	Many N children grow up feeling detached and misunderstood by their S parent.
S parents can ground their imaginative N child through their practical focus on facts and details.	By focusing on facts and details, S parents may stifle their N child's ability to explore hunches or alternative possibilities. This could create boredom/indifference.
S parents can demonstrate the value of experience and using one's senses.	S parents can cause confusion and/or isolation if the N child does not have the opportunity to share their way of perceiving information.

Treasure Tools and Tips for the Sensing parent to use with their Intuitive child

1. Allow the Intuitive child to explore new concepts using existing knowledge. This helps them put their learnings into practice; they might not like to repeat their learning in the same way that you do.
2. In your child's search for meaning, he/she might not notice or remember the facts and details. Remember the Intuitive child is looking for the 'big picture'. Stretch yourself to look at longer-term, future possibilities with them.
3. The Intuitive child will often seek new information and conceptual ideas to see and understand the outcomes of a situation. Understand that they are not 'ditzy' or strange; they just see the world differently from you.
4. As a Sensing parent, you can help your Intuitive child understand the practicalities of life. But don't force your child to adhere to these Sensing realities all the time, as this will create stress in your child.
5. Allow the Intuitive child the freedom to create, use their imagination and focus on future possibilities. Run with the Intuitive child's ideas. This use of your opposite preference, and understanding of how others function, is good for you too!
6. Many Intuitive children feel detached from their Sensing parents when the parent fails to connect with or understand the child's view of the world. Follow the Intuitive child's ideas and dreams initially – you can always provide a reality check later. Learn and change!
7. Discuss ways to relate to your child with Intuitive friends. They can give you alternative ideas on how to understand your child and provide the stimulation and freedom of mind that the Intuitive child enjoys.
8. Encourage your Intuitive child to share independent discussions with your Intuitive friends. You don't need to be there.
9. When working on projects or ideas with your Intuitive child, get them to practise looking at practical steps to get to their main idea. But don't spent too long doing this or they will get bored.

WHO IS THIS MONSTER (OR TREASURE) IN MY HOUSE?

Golden nuggets of wisdom found

Summarise your thoughts

CHAPTER 11

THINKING – FEELING PARENT/CHILD RELATIONSHIPS

In this chapter, we're going to look at **Thinking (T) - Feeling (F) parent/child relationships**. This chapter is about how you and your child form decisions - your decision-making process:

FEELING (F) PARENT WITH THINKING (T) CHILD

Harmony versus logic

I wish I was a Thinker.
When my Thinking daughter bought her last computer, she was aware that she was solely responsible for the purchase. I rejoiced. Finally, my children were paying their way. I had this parenting gig right! Then out of left field came, 'Mum, when you paid for Jack's last computer you paid $500 more than you did for my last computer.' Her logical, critiquing statements hit their target. Wow, I thought, not even an, 'I don't want to upset you, but...' or 'I know that you have always been so generous, but...' That's how I would have started the conversation - with a softer, more diplomatic opening. Her blunt approach hurt me. My husband and I always

endeavoured to keep money matters even between our two children. I instinctively wanted to retaliate, and blurted out, 'But I thought that you were doing this yourself?' She responded, 'Don't worry about it. If you don't want me to have the same as Jack, that's okay.'

Cassie was homing in on the concept of 'fair and reasonable', but her comment left me feeling guilty and sad. I hated the idea that she thought I might care about one of my children more than the other. I always want them to feel equally loved, and don't want to hurt anyone's feelings or cause disharmony. But Cassie didn't seem to be getting emotional at all. She spoke to me in a calm and direct way as I listened to her objective, analytical breakdown of the events that surrounded the last purchase of computers. She challenged my memory about the details, such as the price of Jack's last computer and hers, and the fact that he was older than her when he received it. She pointed out why forking out $500 to her was the 'right' thing for me to do. And she got it! After all, it was the only answer to her logical analysis of the situation.

Table 9: treasures and troubles of the F parent and the T child

TREASURES	TROUBLES
The F parent can teach the T child to use their empathy as well as their thinking when making decisions.	The F parent will often think that their T child is uncaring and lacks sensitivity. Their T child may think their F parent is soft!
The F parent can guide their T child to see someone else's point of view.	Sometimes the F parent can feel that their T child's logical thought processes are harsh and judgemental.
The F parent will use their empathetic skills when dealing with the T child. Even though they might not agree with their child, they are always trying to help them to see the 'good' in others.	The F parent will worry about their T child hurting other people's feelings. They can be disillusioned by the fact that their child is not on the same page.
The F parent talks about 'who' and shows concern and interest in people. They can explain how to interpret people's emotional cues and teach the T child ways to respond so that they have relationship skills in this area.	The F parent dislikes being asked 'Why?' and questioned about things that they have said or done as though they are wrong. The T child feels detached when too much focus is on people's emotional needs.
The F parent often makes Feeling statements and demonstrates concern about others to their T child. This helps the T child to express their own emotions.	The F parent is often not ready for the reaction of disbelief, irony or disagreement that they get from the T child when they make a Feeling statement.
The F parent will counsel and reprimand their T child using value and harmony as their preferred reasoning.	The T child requires facts and logic and often can feel misunderstood by their F parent.
The T child's need for logic and questioning can help the F parent see another perspective that is important and helpful for communicating with other Types.	The F parent does not see the T child's need for logic. They overwhelm the T child with emotion. The T child can disagree with the parent's seemingly illogical point of view.

Treasure Tools and Tips for the Feeling parent to use with their Thinking child

1. The Feeling parent thinks about how decisions affect others and often worries that their Thinking child is unfeeling. This is not so. When dealing with Thinking children, ask first of all, 'Is it logical and fair?' Remember that once the Thinker has expressed their initial Thinking thought, they can follow up quickly with a Feeling thought.
2. The Feeling parent's most effective way of communicating with their Thinking child is to speak their 'language'. Be non-emotional and fair in your delivery. Make sure to have the correct information. The Thinking child is like your 'fact police'. They will always have their facts straight about what has been previously said or done.
3. Thinking children will look at what is wrong before noticing what is right. They often need to have this pointed out to them, as it is important to remind them about the positive things in life. Ask them how they would like positive comments to be made to them or about them. You might find it is very different from your own preference.
4. Don't get emotionally involved when the Thinking child is angry or annoyed with you. Wait until they have calmed down and then be logical, reasonable, precise and concise with your follow-up discussion of the dispute. Accept critical feedback without taking it personally. Use this feedback to improve the way you communicate with your Thinking child.
5. The Thinking child will usually try to negotiate their way out of a deal or into one. Have your facts and logic ready before you do battle over any topic – whether it's about money, homework, social life, household rules or anything else.
6. The Thinking child finds it hard to respond to texts and emails from Feeling people with the appropriate amount of warmth. I have taught my children, both of whom are Thinkers, how to write a text or email back to a Feeling person. For them it is hard work to put positive, affirming words together when they would rather

THINKING – FEELING PARENT/CHILD RELATIONSHIPS

> be succinct and logical. They are willing to do it, however, as they are aware of other people's Types and perceptions.
> 7. The Thinking child enjoys praise, as we all do. However, do not use emotive, empathetic words that might overwhelm them and make them feel, as my children say, 'slightly sick'. Simple praise such as 'great work', 'good job' and 'you have worked really well' all work.
> 8. Trusting that your parents are fair, consistent and logical is the ultimate Thinking child/Feeling parent relationship. Honesty is important to the Thinking child, and if they find out that you have lied, trust will take forever to rebuild. So tell the truth.
> 9. Feeling parents should keep their highly emotional responses to events (crying, et cetera) private until their emotions have settled, as the Thinking child might be overcome/frightened/stressed and unable to handle their own emotional responses to the situation.

WHO IS THIS MONSTER (OR TREASURE) IN MY HOUSE?

Golden nuggets of wisdom found

Summarise your thoughts

FEELING (F) PARENT WITH FEELING (F) CHILD

Harmony with harmony

Self-care comes first.

Sarah and Anna are mother and daughter Feeling Types who love to support and care for people. Anna would sometimes come home from school hurt and upset by other children's behaviour. Her way of interacting with children was to be generous, giving and kind, but she was often rebuffed. Rather than encourage her daughter to reflect on whether she was annoying other children by being interfering, or was misinterpreting the other children's remarks, Sarah's automatic response was to tell Anna to avoid these groups of children. Without checking the truth of the situation, Sarah agreed with Anna's opinion that they were mean, spiteful and unkind. As a result, Anna went through friendship groups like wildfire. Rather than persevere and learn how to handle different people, she focused only on people's negative responses to what she perceived as her gifts of giving. As human beings we all have our feelings hurt at some stage during our lives, regardless of whether we are Thinking or Feeling Types. But Feeling Types have less resilience to the logical, critiquing language of the Thinking person.

Sarah and Anna will often help others without being asked. This is wonderful; however, they often complain that no-one acknowledges or thanks them for their kind gestures. As a result, they feel unappreciated and this affects their emotional health and resilience. As a parent, Sarah can help both herself and Anna recognise that kind gestures need to be given without emotional ties; that it *is* okay not to be thanked. To do this, they must both question their purpose. Why are they helping others? Is it simply to help other people in an altruistic way, or so they can be emotionally rewarded by the recipient's gratitude? If it's the latter, Sarah and Anna may end up being hurt. By learning to analyse their motives, they will be able to make choices about giving themselves emotionally to others. It is important for the Feeler's self-worth and happiness to make choices and draw boundaries around who to help, who to be friends with and why.

Knowledge of the differences between Thinking and Feeling will help build resilience, and give both Types the tools to look after both their own feelings and the expectations of others.

Table 10: treasures and troubles of the F parent and the F child

TREASURES	TROUBLES
The F parent and F child will be sensitive to each other's feelings and needs. They will create a harmonious environment for themselves and others.	F parents are often unaware of personality differences, and fail to help the F child acknowledge and understand the differences between the Thinking and Feeling approaches to life.
The F parent and F child will understand each other's values and try to maintain equilibrium.	The desire for equilibrium can fail to build resilience in the F child, and conversations with Thinkers may hurt their feelings and make them unhappy.
Both F parent and F child love to help create harmony in the household.	The F parent will often commiserate with their F child, rather than helping them to understand the differing views and point out the different thought processes of other members of the household. This can see the family divided into separate 'camps'.
The F parent will help their child build friendships around people and values.	Sometimes both F parent and F child can martyr themselves in their desire to keep up 'happy' appearances. They may be deeply unhappy at the same time because they are not being acknowledged in the way they would like.
The F parent and F child will both feel loved and connected to each other.	The F parent and F child will be unable to cope with the way that Thinking Types relate to them if they give emotionally and always expect a positive response.
The F parent will confirm and encourage their F child's value-based and harmonious approach towards problem solving.	The F parent and F child's desire to help others is often at the expense of their own feelings.
The F parent and F child are both demonstrative in their emotions. They can cry and laugh easily, and the F parent creates an environment where it is safe to do so.	The F parent may fail to teach the F child that sometimes uninhibited emotional expression is inappropriate. F children who cry easily may be labelled a 'cry baby'.

Treasure Tools and Tips for the Feeling parent to use with their Feeling child

1. Providing that the Feeling parent and Feeling child share the same values, they will be able to co-operate and appreciate each other's actions and language. So go ahead and love them with your natural gifts of empathy and sensitivity, but try to stretch them occasionally by exposing them to the logical, critiquing language they will experience in the Thinking world.
2. The Feeling parent and child will be sensitive to other people's needs and emotions and give accordingly. You both need to be aware that if doing so makes you feel resentful or powerless, you can change your behaviour. You are in charge of your own emotions and how much you give.
3. Both parent and child often selflessly help others and can end up feeling used if their need for being valued is not met. Parental self-reflection is important so that, as a Feeling parent, you can show your Feeling child how to love and take care of themselves and build resilience and happiness.
4. The Feeling parent and child may not have the emotional strength to handle the logical conversations of the Thinkers in their lives. Teach yourself and your child how to handle people who think and express themselves differently from you. Discuss your learnings from this book and apply them to your lives.
5. Feeling children love to help and create harmony in the household. They will try to keep family relationships between parents and siblings on an even keel, even if it means putting their happiness in jeopardy. Teach them (and yourself) that taking care of yourself is the number one priority, because you can't help others if you are in emotional deficit yourself.
6. Feeling parents encourage the Feeling child to focus on the values and people-based decision-making process that is natural for these children. You should explain the benefits that a Thinker's logical, critiquing decision making can bring to their lives. Both ways of making decisions are important and valuable.

THINKING – FEELING PARENT/CHILD RELATIONSHIPS

7. Feeling parents and children can build their resilience to logical, direct conversations, which may seem abrasive or invasive, by discussing and working out their responses in advance. This will give them confidence.
8. The Feeling child may be more prone to outward shows of emotions, such as hugging, kissing and crying in front of others. This of course is fine, but the Feeling parent may need to discuss with the Feeling child how to express emotions in public to avoid being teased or making others uncomfortable.
9. Help build your Feeling child's emotional well-being by allowing them to develop their supportive, nurturing strengths. Show them how they can positively touch the lives of others, but make sure that they have support systems to help them decompress when their own emotions become too much for them.

THINKING (T) PARENT WITH FEELING (F) CHILD

Logic with harmony

Why are we always fighting?
For many years, I have witnessed first-hand how the Type differences of my Thinking friend, Tim, and his Feeling daughter, Jo, cause havoc in their relationship. The way they use language has seen their conversations become unintentional battles. His language is questioning, logical and analytic. Hers is people centred, empathetic and focused on what is best for the person in question.

As time has gone by, Jo has begun to feel upset that her feelings and achievements are never appreciated or recognised. Tim is busy telling her how she could improve instead of supporting her and complimenting her on the things that she has achieved. Tim's favourite saying is, 'Nobody remembers second.' When Jo won running races at school, instead of praising his daughter, Tim would offer what he thought was constructive criticism, such as, 'Great race, but you need to practise more and see if you can knock another ten seconds off your time.' Where was the unconditional love and pride in a job well done?

Jo feels picked on and that her achievements are never properly acknowledged. Tim in turn is puzzled and annoyed by her reactive behaviour. As he sees it, he is only trying to help her improve but she gets emotional all the time. How can she get better if she doesn't look objectively at what she's doing and fix it? It has reached the stage where Jo feels that her father is always 'mean and angry', and she can only handle him for short periods. Tim cannot understand what he has done 'wrong' and has become more impatient and scathing in his communication with her. They genuinely love each other, but are both blind to their Type preferences.

Table 11: treasures and troubles of the T parent and the F child

TREASURES	TROUBLES
The T parent can build the F child's resilience by helping them understand the differences between their thought processes.	The T parent's logical viewpoints may offend and upset the F child's values and feelings if the child doesn't understand that their parent's thought processes are different from their own.
The T parent can share their viewpoint with their F child so that the child understands that T people are not being mean when they ask questions and probe the child's opinions and decisions, but just have different ways of thinking.	The T parent's constant critiquing and questioning of decisions can cause the F child to feel distressed and upset.
T parents can show that their logical thought processes are different from their child's and discuss the value of both their style of thinking and their child's.	The F child often feels that the T parent appears angry with them, even when this is not the case.
T parents may question or disagree with the F child's point of view in order to help them see the logical side of a discussion.	The F child feels very uncomfortable in the face of conflict, whether it is real or imagined.
The T parent can show their F child how straightforward thinking can take the complexity out of emotional situations.	The T parent's language may not resonate with the F child, who may then feel unloved.
The T parent is able to get to the point quickly and without emotion.	T parents may find emotion uncomfortable and will often be unable to deal effectively with the F child's need for emotional support.
T parents can demonstrate that the 'likeability' factor in making decisions may not always be as important as honesty and truth.	T parents may experience conflict with their teenage F child as peers become more influential and the F child seeks peer approval and emotional connection.

Treasure Tools and Tips for the Thinking parent to use with their Feeling child

1. The Thinking parent's logical viewpoint will often offend the Feeling child's values. Explain your different thought processes and show them that you are not trying to hurt their feelings.
2. The Feeling child will sometimes feel unloved and misunderstood as the Thinking parent will not appear to care about them in the way that they would like. Give them the hugs, praise and personal reassurance they require to show that they are loved.
3. The Thinker's need for critiquing and questioning others' ideas and decisions is often seen by the Feeling child as evidence that their parent is angry or upset, even though this is not necessarily true. This distresses the Feeler, who seeks harmony. Discuss your differences and ask how you can best fulfil those emotional needs.
4. The Feeling child needs affirmation and recognition for the good deeds they do and the compassion they show for others. The Thinking parent does not usually recognise this, as they are not in the same headspace. Be aware of this and act on it by providing recognition and praise.
5. Feeling children's need for harmony and emotional well-being can make them sensitive to the direct, blunt conversation of Thinking Types. Helping them understand other people's conversations can put the Thinking conversations into perspective for them.
6. If the Feeling child is emotive over an issue that the Thinking parent perceives as unimportant, the parent's reaction can sound angry. They might say something like, 'That was nothing, and you should not get upset.' Do not dismiss the Feeling child's sentiments. Be prepared to understand and respond in kind to their perspective. Say something like, 'I understand that you are feeling sad. How can I help you?'
7. The Feeling child would prefer to smooth things over, rather than face conflict. They can be the 'glue' that keeps the family together. If their siblings or parents are upset, the Feeling child will attempt to 'fix' the situation, even if it means giving up something that is

THINKING – FEELING PARENT/CHILD RELATIONSHIPS

valuable to them (such as toys, food or, as they get older, their time). Be aware of this and help them cope with other people's emotions. Give them strategies to keep themselves in a caring but neutral position.
8. The Feeling child will often 'put up' with their Thinking parent, but resentment and anger can build despite their desire for harmony. Be aware of this potential conflict as they may detach themselves from you emotionally and leave the relationship. Use your personality knowledge early to save years of emotional damage.
9. The Thinking parent can teach their child how and when they should express themselves in a more direct way.

WHO IS THIS MONSTER (OR TREASURE) IN MY HOUSE?

Golden nuggets of wisdom found

Summarise your thoughts

THINKING (T) PARENT WITH THINKING (T) CHILD

Logic with logic

I am always right – just try me!
Dinner time at our house is a mixed bag of opinionated conversations. From their early teen years, Jack and Cassie have regularly sparred with each other, and Paul, over the dinner table. As my young Thinkers were forming their views about friends, schooling and life, they had many heated conversations with their outspoken Thinking father, who had a more old-fashioned belief system. As the years have passed, these discussions have embraced more mature topics such as jobs, business and marriage. The discussions that ensue are lively to say the least and, much to my dismay, often do not end on a harmonious note. I like to finish my meal in peace and harmony, not in the midst of three rather hostile parties facing off across the table!

But I have learned that expressing opinions in their preferred communication style is important to my family, and that what I interpret as rude or blunt, they simply see as the truth. Telling the truth as they all see it, from three viewpoints, gives rise to a conversation that is often a blunt, straightforward barrage of critical words. However, at the end of the day, if they fail to win over the other 'combatants' with their point of view, they agree to disagree. Nobody wants to hurt anybody's feelings. All three of them will walk away from the table calmly, each knowing that, deep down, they were right all along! And I have learned to remain calm while the chaos rages, knowing that we all love and respect each other.

Remember, no matter what Type they are, everyone's feelings should be respected. Tact is paramount! It is okay if you always think that you are right. Just keep it to yourself!

Table 12: treasures and troubles of the T parent and the T child

TREASURES	TROUBLES
Both T parent and T child are on the same page with their values around honesty and fairness.	Even though they both use straightforward, logical language, the Thinkers can still upset each other with their unfiltered honesty.
The T parent and T child will often enjoy making decisions together as they are likeminded with their logical decision-making style and questioning mind.	The T parent will not encourage empathy/personal values in their child's decision making. The T child may lack an understanding of the impact of their decisions on other people and relationships.
The T parent and T child will both remain objective about situations.	Being likeminded, they will both like being right and this can cause conflict, both between them and/or with other people.
Both the T parent and T child are able to analyse situations and problems, but are not always able to understand the emotional factors.	T parents don't always encourage their T child to put themselves into someone else's shoes and this lack of empathy can offend and upset others.
T parents and the T child are able to take the emotion out of decisions.	Sometimes both T parents and T children are unable to identify and understand the emotional level of a conversation and they can become stressed or dismissive. They may appear cold and heartless.
T parents and T children are 'straight shooters'. They will let people know the lay of the land without embellishment.	T parents and T children may sometimes offend and upset people with their straight talk, including other Thinking Types. Thinkers can often unwittingly give their critical, logical opinions without considering others' feelings.
Both T parent and T child are constantly questioning and assessing situations, which is motivated by their desire to increase their knowledge and competence.	T parents' and T children's emotional awareness can be stunted if their Feeling side is not explored and used as well.

Treasure Tools and Tips for the Thinking parent to use with their Thinking child

1. The Thinking parent and child are often on the same page in terms of language and expectations. However, this does not mean that they are in total harmony. Often, they are far from it. These two Thinking preferences are always asking 'Why?' and can annoy each other by constantly questioning each other's opinions. Be aware that as the adult in this situation, you need to listen thoughtfully to your child's opinion before expressing your own. Consistently clarify with them that people are not always right or wrong … they just have different thoughts and ideas.
2. When making decisions, the Thinking Type's initial thinking process is logical, which can lead to a lack of emotive input. It is the adult Thinker's responsibility to model how to see the world from the Feeling Type's perspective, and therefore help their Thinking child understand the very different approaches the two Types have when making decisions.
3. The Thinker parent and child will be able to stay objective about situations and not get emotionally involved, which can be a blessing. It helps them form an objective point of view on a situation. But it can also be a curse, as they may not appear to care about the emotions that different situations arouse in others. Work on this, and discuss with Feeling Types what kinds of actions they can take if someone is upset.
4. Thinkers can avoid working on relationships, as this can be an area of stress for them. But doing so gives you a chance to teach the Thinking child the value of being able to share emotions positively, both physically and verbally.
5. Both parent and child need to recognise that it is okay to lose an argument and that life will continue if you do. They need to learn to lose an argument gracefully. Role modelling might be very important in this area! Showing how to lose graciously in sport or other games can also be helpful.

6. Apologising can be hard for the Thinker, and sometimes they will refuse to say sorry if they do not mean it. It is important to explain to the Thinking child (and adult) that they are not always right and that admitting they are wrong is important for personal growth.
7. Thinkers need to understand that other people might like support, rather than analysis. It is up to the Thinking parent to be aware of this and to help their child develop a vault of emotionally supportive language to open and use when necessary.
8. The Thinking parent and Thinking child can work together to find a logical process for coping with the emotional responses from others. For example, ask the simple question, 'How can I help you?' and then follow the cues from there. Too often we respond in the way we would like to be responded to instead of asking what people need.
9. The Thinking parent and child have great skills for taking the emotion out of a situation so that they can put it into perspective. This is a natural gift that the Thinking parent can encourage in the Thinking child, even showing them how a Thinker can help another Feeling Type to gain perspective on their life.

Golden nuggets of wisdom found

Summarise your thoughts

CHAPTER 12

JUDGING – PERCEIVING PARENT/ CHILD RELATIONSHIPS

This chapter is about **Judging (J) – Perceiving (P) parent-child relationships**. It is about how you and your child prefer to live your outer lives (your lifestyles):

PERCEIVING (P) PARENT WITH PERCEIVING (P) CHILD

Flexible = flexible

Pushing the envelope.
Clambering into the car after school, my Perceiving daughter, Cassie, tells me that she has organised a play date at a friend's place. Much to the annoyance of my Judging son, Jack, we deviate from the journey home to take her there. After dropping her off, I remember that I have not planned dinner. We stop at the local shops to pick up supplies. Taking a very frustrated Jack home, I begin to prepare the meal. In the midst of this, Cassie calls to be picked up. I put dinner on hold and race out to get her.

In the car on the way home, Cassie looks in her school diary and sees that she has a project to finish that night, and she has not started it yet! Another stop at the shops for project materials, then homeward bound. We are excited and high on adrenalin in anticipation of the imminent, potentially impossible, deadline. Over dinner we discuss the looming project, as our brains feverishly work overtime with excitement. Dinner is finished in a rush, and we move on to researching and writing the assignment! There are a few details that we have to leave out because they will take too much time to investigate. It may not be perfect, but who cares? Perceivers are all about passing, not excellence, and if they do achieve excellence, all the better.

By 11pm the project is finished, dishes are done, and we fall into bed shattered. As I lie there, I think about the day and the over-the-top pace that we put ourselves through. On reflection, I contemplate the importance for me to practise, teach and reinforce the habits of scheduling, following plans and meeting deadlines. It is important that the Perceiving parent emphasises these skills as they are an everyday part of our Judging world. Without these habits in place, the Perceiver's lives will be a roller coaster of adrenaline highs that will eventually exhaust them ... I promise to start that tomorrow!

Table 13: treasures and troubles of the P parent and the P child

TREASURES	TROUBLES
P parents are not too concerned about the P child's belongings being neat and tidy, so there's not too much nagging.	There is often disregard for the value of order and being organised, and without parental direction the P child often misses out on understanding that in a Judging world these are important skills to have.
Both P parent and P child are able to fit into each other's flexible timetables and move things around to suit each other without this being an issue.	The P parent's flexibility around time frames with work, projects and life in general does not always prepare the P child for the less flexible Judging world that we live in. The child may unintentionally appear selfish when they expect others to change their plans.
Both Ps can fit extra activities into the daily timetable. This allows them to take advantage of valuable learning opportunities and unusual life experiences.	Both P parent and P child can pack too much into their impulsive schedules and end up stressed, overloaded and messy.
Both P parent and P child are excited by the last-minute dash at most things in life, whether that involves work or play. Deadlines do not stress them. Rather, they thrive on them.	P parents are casual and inconsistent about keeping an appointment diary and making lists. The child may miss important appointments such as dental check-ups or fail to be prepared for, and therefore miss, planned events such as school excursions.
The P parent does not always put their P child under pressure to make sure important tasks are a priority, such as school diaries being signed, notices brought home, lunch boxes unpacked, et cetera.	P parents sometimes forget notices/diaries and appointments. This does not provide a good role model for their P child if it is habitual.
P parents and their P child are not usually concerned about sticking strictly to social arrangements. They are more relaxed about play dates, start and finish times for activities, and remembering significant dates.	P parents can allow their P child to think that being late/forgetting arrangements/rushing in at the last minute is acceptable. They need to know that this can cause conflict and friction in future relationships and the workplace.
P parents allow unimportant things to slide and will have 'grey' areas around most decisions.	There may be little preparation for the adult Judging world, where bills and credit card balances have to be paid on time. Penalties will occur for being late.

Treasure Tools and Tips for the Perceiving parent to use with their Perceiving child

1. Although the Perceiving parent may not be concerned about the 'puddles of stuff' that the child will leave around the house, it is important to model cleaning up and putting things in their place. Without being taught these skills, the naturally disorganised P child could find themselves living in chaos. Persist in getting them to tidy up often. This is a good habit for you both.
2. Perceiving parents will allow flexible time frames for jobs or tasks to be completed, often changing the deadline to suit both themselves and their Perceiving child. Teach your child that this is not always possible and that many deadlines in life cannot be changed.
3. Both Perceiving parent and child will be happy to slot extra activities into their day (even when they are busy). This is more stimulating for them than the 'tedious' scheduled day. Both of you need to avoid putting too much into your day and becoming overwhelmed and stressed.
4. It is important for the Perceiving parent to educate their Perceiving child about being on time for appointments in the 'real world'. Being aware of your own Type means that you can help the child understand and develop these life skills. Try to model punctuality for appointments outside the home, even if it goes against Type.
5. Perceiving children are much more accepting of the second supermarket run and other last-minute, emergency activities. However, they need to learn how to be organised in a Judging world, so write the supermarket list together, and let your Perceiving child tick items off as you go.
6. Model the Judging skills that are important in your Perceiving child's world, such as being on time for school, getting assignments in on time and studying for exams.
7. Find out what it is that your child would like to have as a special treat. Use this as a 'carrot' to reward them when they finish a task on time. It will need to be something they are willing to work for.
8. Include structure and timelines in your daily life and help the

Perceiving child to recognise the importance of these processes in family, school and work. This will help them fit into the parameters of societal expectations. It is a Judging world!
9. Keep a whiteboard in the family area where everyone's tasks and assignments can be seen. You can check it together regularly and help to alert each other when deadlines are near. Just don't forget to update it!

WHO IS THIS MONSTER (OR TREASURE) IN MY HOUSE?

Golden nuggets of wisdom found

Summarise your thoughts

JUDGING (J) PARENT WITH PERCEIVING (P) CHILD

Planned versus flexible

You are a parent for the rest of your life.
My mother is a wonderful Judging mum to four Perceiving children. She is well organised and always has a schedule. She became a single mum when we hit our teens, but she still managed to keep up with all of our timetables, homework and social lives. Out of the four of us, I was the messiest. I never put things back in their appropriate places (I still don't today), left clothes lying around, and borrowed things without bothering to return them! I would often forget where I left things and my mother would patiently help me look for them. Her favourite saying was, 'You would forget your head if it wasn't screwed on.' She was right; even today in her mid-eighties, she checks her house before I leave to make sure that I don't leave anything behind. How lucky are we to have such a patient, kind, Judging mum to learn from? I too hate mess, but I can't seem to stop creating it, so I do my best to use my Judging side of Type every day in my own Perceiving way.

Table 14: treasures and troubles of the J parent and the P child

TREASURES	TROUBLES
J parents keep the P child's life in order by scheduling activities in a regular way, keeping their belongings tidy and sticking to a daily routine.	J parents don't understand the need for flexibility and the excitement that spontaneity brings to the P child's life. The P child may become despondent or bored with the constant ordered approach or controlling nature of the J parent.
J parents can teach their P child how to live in a J world.	The J parents may put too much pressure on the P child, who is already working against his/her true preferences.
J parents can help their P child to organise and schedule schoolwork, projects and other activities, and ensures they meet deadlines.	A J parent's frustration and anger can be triggered when the P child responds to situations with what, to the J parent, appears to be procrastination when finishing homework/tasks or meeting commitments. The P child enjoys the rush of approaching deadlines and may not understand the constant nagging of their J parent.
J parents can show their P child how to focus on the individual steps required to achieve a goal.	The J parent's ordered approach to achievement compared with their P child's haphazard lifestyle can lead to disagreement and/or a sense of failure for both.
J parents can show their P child the value of discipline, being on time and getting on in life.	J parents become frustrated when their P child does not appear to value or adhere to their organisation and structure. The P child feels pressured and conflicted.
J parents are quick to make decisions and proceed with action, which counterbalances the P child's often too relaxed timing and decision making.	J parents make quick decisions once they have the necessary information, whereas the P child likes to mull over all of the options before arriving at a decision. This can make the P child feel rushed or overwhelmed.
In order to create closure, J parents will make decisions on behalf of their P child.	P children may fail to develop a sense of autonomy and/or feel disempowered if they are not allowed to make their own decisions.

Treasure Tools and Tips for the Judging parent to use with their Perceiving child

1. The Perceiving child can be the bane of the Judging parent's life, as they have little care for schedules and timetables. Discuss with your Perceiving child the importance of these and chunk their learning into one or two areas of their life where these structures are important. For example, getting to school on time and having homework finished by the deadline set. Once one good habit has formed, try another.
2. Understand that the Perceiving child may start many tasks without finishing any of them until the need arises. Even then, the task may not be finished to the degree of perfection that satisfies the Judging parent. Moderate your expectation of perfection, and if this results in poor school work, untidy rooms, not being on time, et cetera, let the Perceiving child wear the consequences. Experience can be the greatest teacher for you both.
3. The J parent works steadily towards a goal in order to finish on time. The Perceiving child will leave their work until the last minute as projects or assignments only become interesting or imperative when the deadline is fast approaching – or even on top of them! Understanding your different approaches to study will help you guide your child to achieve their best results without stamping your values and work style on them.
4. If the Judging parent is able to recognise and understand their differences, they can teach the Perceiving child strategies to help them keep order in their world.
5. The Judging parent will usually have school notes and diaries signed and returned on time, unless the Perceiving child has left them in their bag or at school somewhere. They can help diarise and prioritise important dates and times for their Perceiving child.
6. The Perceiving child requires some time without structure or commitments, when they can drift between unfinished activities without retribution (even if it means leaving a trail of chaos in their wake). As a Judging parent, it is important to recognise your child's

natural stress-free zone and give them time to be themselves.
7. The Judging parent usually has strict rules and values that they adhere to. They will stand by their methods of discipline. Remember that there are times when rules can be broken, and this is not a bad thing.
8. Be aware that the Perceiving child requires a range of choices in areas such as activities, school topics, clothing, friends and food. Having just one option is frustrating for them. If the P child suggests another option, let them go with it. Choices are as important to them as quick decisions are to the Judging parent. Having choices allows them to feel happy and comfortable with their decisions.
9. The Judging parent may be appalled and upset by the Perceiving child's messy bedroom. As the teen years approach, it may be helpful to simply close the door and ignore the chaos. There may be other, more important battles to fight with your Perceiving child, and it's important not to exhaust yourself and frustrate your child by micro-managing every aspect of their life. As the saying goes, 'Pick your battles.'

JUDGING (J) PARENT WITH JUDGING (J) CHILD

Planner = planned

Let's stick to the plan.
My sister-in-law and her youngest daughter are both Judging Types – they flourish on schedules and timetables and stick to them beautifully. When visiting, I always look at the family's board of programmed after-school activities and nearly die! It is a running joke – while I always seem to be busy, none of that 'busyness' is planned. But my sister-in-law's children each have three or four after-school activities locked into an air-tight schedule that never deviates. Both mum and daughter interweave the weekly after-school activities, which include swimming, water polo, netball, dance and violin practice, not to mention fitting in a nutritious home-cooked dinner. My Perceiving brother and niece get swept up in the tide of motion as these two energetic, focused females organise the whole family and 'make stuff happen'.

As a Perceiving person watching my sister-in-law and her Judging daughter in action, I am in awe. I don't want to be them, but I am so impressed with how much they get done and their determination to get things organised and done the right way. They run their lives like a well-oiled machine. These are the people who keep families and workplaces running in an orderly, well-managed system. We could not be without them in our lives. Not right or wrong – just different gifts and talents.

Table 15: treasures and troubles of the J parent and the J child

TREASURES	TROUBLES
J parents and the J child prefer order and structure and are happy in a household where things are in their place.	Messy, disorganised environments may create stress for the J child. They may not be able to cope in a school or work environment that is chaotic, but over which they have no control.
Both J parent and J child enjoy knowing schedules ahead of time and planning daily activities.	J parents cannot always provide the J child with the skills to 'recalibrate' when things don't go as planned.
J parents establish clear rules and boundaries, which children like, as they feel secure in a stable environment. The J child will feel especially comfortable with this.	The fixed order and structure that J parents provide for the J child does not allow for the ever-changing reality of life. Spontaneity and a more flexible approach is sometimes required.
Judging parents are able to help their J child plan and execute their tasks on time, giving them both a great sense of satisfaction.	J parents don't foster resilience for life's unexpected 'curveballs'. Their J children may not learn how to 'think on their feet'.
The J parent and J child enjoy making decisions quickly and will achieve much.	Both the J parent's and J child's quick decision-making skills can be too fast to accommodate additional information that could change the outcome of important decisions.
Both J parent and J child enjoy completing one task at a time.	The J parent may not prepare the J child for the modern world of work, where there may be competing demands that require multitasking and working on several projects at once.
J parents are usually firm disciplinarians, who have rules and expectations around behaviour and work ethic.	J parents sometimes cannot see the 'grey' area of a situation, and may stick to their rules just to make a point.

Treasure Tools and Tips for the Judging parent to use with their Judging child

1. Judging Types like to be in control. They usually have set ideas and schedules and find that altering them can be stressful. As we all know, last-minute changes are a part of everyday life, so coping mechanisms need to be discussed and put into place for both you and your child.
2. If the two Judging Types have different beliefs and ideas about how things should be done, conflict may occur. This happens because you both feel so right about your opinions and decisions that neither of you welcome new or conflicting data or are willing to negotiate. Parental modelling of 'active' listening and negotiation skills should be taught and utilised.
3. The Judging parent, like the Judging child, likes to come to an agreement about any future goals as quickly as possible. They like to wrap up the plan so that they can get on with implementing it. However, this desire for fast decision making can mean that you both overlook other factors that could make a difference to the end result. Create the practice of more information gathering before decisions are made.
4. Judging parents and children like to have clear rules and procedures. The clarity of these structures, whether it be discipline, tasks or schoolwork, is useful to both of you but does not always prepare the Judging child for the unpredictability of life. Make a game of making some last-minute, spontaneous decisions and following through with them. Reflect on how it made you feel and plan to throw your schedule out once a week or once a month, just for the hell of it.
5. Judging parents and children enjoy planning tasks in advance and need to follow these tasks through until they reach completion. This gives both of you great satisfaction and confidence when something is completed because you can then move on to the next task. Teach your Judging child the processes that you find

beneficial as a Judging adult, such as using a diary, planner or other scheduling tools.
6. If someone disrupts the process of their well-thought-out plans, the Judging parent and child become stressed. It is up to you as the Judging parent to help your child recalibrate and understand that change is not the end of the world. Show them that re-working ideas can still produce great results, maybe even better ones. Change does not always mean starting from scratch. They can often re-use some of their previous plan to rebuild an idea or activity.
7. Effective use of time is very important to Judging people, who can feel very frustrated or 'down' when nothing is achieved or shown for the time they put into something. Encourage your child to look for other ways and ideas to put their valuable time to use.
8. The Judging child enjoys organising other people, but this can make them appear bossy and turn other children away. Teach them how to use their direction as a skill. To become a good leader, they need to listen to others and also follow others' leads when appropriate.
9. Judging children often like to do one thing at a time, finishing one task before starting the next. When they know the underlying structure is in place that gives them a baseline to work from, introduce a variety of topics.

PERCEIVING (P) PARENT WITH JUDGING (J) CHILD

Flexible versus planner

Sort me out, please.
As a Perceiving parent, I cannot count the number of times I have turned back home for the forgotten lunch or consent form, not to mention the rushed visits for appointments that I have forgotten about and only remembered at the last minute.

At the age of twelve, my Judging son, Jack, took me in hand. We were overseas and we had missed the first boarding call for our flight, probably because I was too busy chattering away to some new 'friend' that Cassie and I had met in the check-in queue. I jumped out of my skin when our names were called over the loud speaker. As I rushed with the family in tow towards our gate, I noticed that Jack was lagging behind. I turned to tell him to hurry up and noticed that he was dragging my huge overnight bag behind him. I had left it under the table in the café where I had been sitting. Thank goodness! And lucky me to have such a treasure travelling with me.

Ever since then, if Jack is with me, he will always check to see if I've left something behind as I get up and leave my seat, and has often picked up a jacket or bag I have left behind as I walk out of a café or restaurant with my head elsewhere. He is like my PA. He will check my diary and remind me, in advance, of any events that I have coming up. As he got older, one of his Judging friends would often text him about school events, such as dress-up days, mission day, parent-teacher meetings and so forth, before we left for school. This would give me the time to organise myself before we went out. I really can remember most things, but it is a joy to have that added support.

I have a son who prefers a structured and decided lifestyle, and he has a mum who enjoys a more flexible and adaptable one, but we are both able to enjoy each other's differences because we understand and accept them.

Table 16: treasures and troubles of the P parent and the J child

TREASURES	TROUBLES
P parents help the J child by 'stretching' them and helping them understand that the world is not always 'in order'. This might not be comfortable, but diversity is part of life.	P parents create stress for the J child due to a lack of order in the household and timetables.
P parents are able to be flexible enough to fit into the J child's schedule, even if they have other things planned.	P parents' continual changing of plans creates a stressful environment for their J child.
P parents are happy to go with the flow so that the J child does not usually have a stressed out, over-organised parent in tow.	The J child feels anxious and out of control when their routines are disturbed, or the P parent is late or has forgotten to do something.
P parents can help the J child learn that not everything goes to plan.	P parents often forget to warn about changes of plans, which may result in arguments and discord.
P parents are not only able to help their J child to be more flexible, but they also teach them to take responsibility for structuring their own lives in the way that makes them happy.	P parents do not appear to value the same rules that their J child lives by; this can cause rifts in their relationship.
The P parent's ability to manage without rules and structure can help the J child be aware that change is an inevitable part of life.	The P parent's ever-changing lifestyle can be perceived by the J child as stressful, and they may feel that their feelings/needs are not a priority. The J child (who likes to control events) may end up feeling they need to parent the parent.
The P parent's tolerance of mess and indifference to housework means the J child can play freely without having to worry about making a mess or upsetting a carefully ordered household.	The P parent's messy environment may create stress for the J child, and their valued belongings may be mislaid or even damaged. They may feel disrespected.

Treasure Tools and Tips for the Perceiving parent to use with their Judging child

1. The Perceiving parent has a flexible approach to time and can go with the flow. This is an important learning experience for the Judging child, as their natural need for order and structure can mean that they struggle with deviations to their routine. If they are exposed to these changes on a daily basis, it will help them adjust to the changes that everyday life brings.
2. The Perceiving parent needs to be aware of the Judging child's need for structure and order, and ensure that they do have a certain amount of structure in their lives. Without this, the Judging child will be stressed and feel out of control. It's all about balance.
3. Planning is also important for the Judging child, and they need to see some formality around the organisation of their days, weekends and other activities. If a Perceiving parent finds this stressful, they can hand over more of the responsibility for organising their schedule/activities to the child. The J child is likely to welcome this.
4. Don't continually change plans that involve the Judging child, as they will become sceptical about any promises that you make.
5. If you do have to change the Judging child's routine, try to give them advance warning. They will have planned around their routine and disruption will cause conflict if it comes out of the blue.
6. In order to get along, Personality Type preferences should be discussed, and opportunities used to work out what each Type's priorities are.
7. As a Perceiving parent, you can provide an outlet for your Judging child's organisational gifts by getting them to teach you strategies for being on time, scheduling your work, et cetera.
8. Help your Judging child develop their full potential by giving them the tools that they need to organise their life, such as milestones, completion dates and progress charts. Celebrate with a ceremony to mark the successful completion of work or sport. These are tools that can help you, too.

9. The Judging child will be aware when others view their Perceiving parent's frequent tardiness and relaxed attitude to life critically. But they will also be grateful for their Perceiving parent's efforts to keep their life in order and be on time for events that are important to the child.

CONCLUSION

Remember that horror story you read at the beginning of the book? The one about the awful school day, and the grumpy children and husband who just couldn't seem to get through a single day without conflict? The one that sounded all too familiar? Well, if you take the information in this book seriously, and really apply it, you just might be able to change the story to something like this…

A GOOD DAY IN A GOOD LIFE

The school morning has started … you are on time because you understand that even though you don't mind being late, it stresses out the rest of your family.

Your son is calmly going about his morning routine at a pace that suits him. He is able to complete his regular tasks to his standard, and as he walks through the kitchen he gives you a quick hug. Your daughter is busy organising her personal life with you. You encourage her to talk while she is packing her lunch and her homework into her bag before brushing her teeth. You and your husband are aware that she enjoys having many friends, so you agree to let her host a weeknight date with two friends, who will leave at dinnertime. Your husband is happy, as he can spend the rest of the evening in peace and quiet.

You bundle your settled, cheery tribe into the car, school bags in tow, and your husband happily drives off. Getting out of the car, both kids wave goodbye and skip into school. You drive away feeling a sense of well-being and love.

After school, the kids clamber into the car. You have established an agreement that the journey home is when you discuss their school day. No phones! Your daughter gets the floor first. She is bursting with news about her latest escapades. She regales you with stories of her friends while your son has time to gather his thoughts. You know that your daughter will talk forever, so you ask her to pop her conversation on hold so your son has a chance to talk. You help him to engage in conversation by asking one question at a time, and allowing time for thought before he answers you. You reflect back his thoughts and ideas, and he feels heard.

With a little bit of work and patience, this can be your new reality. (How good will that be?!)

You arrive home, and your children hang out in the kitchen with you for a snack. Then they sit down to work at the kitchen table, where you are available if they need help. This time is a quiet time, but discussion is always an option if needed. You watch them study and think how lucky you are to have such great kids.

PUT YOUR FAMILY'S TYPE TOGETHER

By working through the information in this book, you will have found your family's Type preferences and formed a Type profile for each member. To help you further, list them below. You can refer back to your and your partner's summary on page 55 and your child/children's summary on page 97.

The integration of the letters creates an amazing overview of who you all are from a personality perspective.

CONCLUSION

1. Name: _____ Type: _____

2. Name: _____ Type: _____

3. Name: _____ Type: _____

4. Name: _____ Type: _____

5. Name: _____ Type: _____

6. Name: _____ Type: _____

7. Name: _____ Type: _____

8. Name: _____ Type: _____

9. Name: _____ Type: _____

10. Name: _____ Type: _____

As mentioned at the beginning of this book, the Myers-Briggs Type Indicator (MBTI) is the true, tested verification of your Personality Type and there are many practitioners, including myself, who are available to help you on your Type journey. If you experienced difficulties in forming a Type profile, you will not be alone. A comprehensive Type profile is a complex concept. I have provided the basics of the MBTI for you, and I hope that you will be inspired to follow your interest in this area to gain a deeper level of understanding. There are many fascinating, informative articles that will broaden your knowledge about Type and the people in your life. (Refer to the Resources section at the back of this book.)

When learning a new concept, we often feel excited and energised, but sometimes we can also be overwhelmed and unsure of where to start. My advice to you is to start unpacking the treasure chest jewel by jewel. In doing so, you will be able to break down the changes that you can see are needed into bite-size chunks of learning and action. See what works and what doesn't. Play around with your changes to see if another approach is better. When you are happy with your progress, take the next step.

Remember, if you make mistakes, most children are relatively forgiving. Your partner may be less so, but with your new lines of communication open, your ability to discuss and understand each other's viewpoint should create love, laughter and forgiveness. We will never be perfect or always right (well, maybe some of us!), but we can enjoy the journey of life with each other if we know who we are and what makes us tick.

Let's take some notes before you leave. What treasures did you discover, and which monsters can you now let go of?

Make a list.

CONCLUSION

TREASURES	TROUBLES

WHO IS THIS MONSTER (OR TREASURE) IN MY HOUSE?

What changes do you need to make to unearth the hidden treasures that lie buried in your relationships with your family, now that you understand the differences and similarities in people's Types?

Now that you know who your monster/treasure is, talk to them with their Personality Type in mind. Start listening. I mean *really* listening. Not listening to respond. Rather, listening to hear and reflect with the other person on *their* conversation, not yours! Don't ever think that one discussion is enough. Every day we are faced with new challenges and changes, and our conversations need to be frequent and positive.

Going forward, change and adapt your pre-set ideas to suit everybody so that you will be on the same page. When you open your eyes and ears to the different Personality Types of the people in your life, you can create monumental change in how you understand and treat others. Working out what motivates and ultimately de-motivates us helps us to clear the monsters of doubt, confusion and unhappiness from our minds.

Learn your theories well but put them aside when you touch the miracle of a living person.

Now, I'm going to leave you with one more important idea. It's possible to stereotype people and box them in when using tools such as the MBTI, so remember that these tools should be used to free up your judgement of others and give you a guide to how other people work.

Remember, we are all unique, and so is our perception of the world and the people in it. In the words of Carl Jung: 'Learn your theories well but put them aside when you touch the miracle of a living person.'

CONNECT WITH ME

Our world can be a very different place if people learn about and understand others – anything is possible and communication is always the key.

So, get talking and listening, share your knowledge and keep learning. There are many wonderful, well-researched MBTI practitioners who have great insights into this topic. You will find them on the internet, along with podcasts and YouTube videos that can give you further education on relationships, communication, resilience and well-being.

On that note, I hope that you have at least begun your personality journey and are fired up to learn more. I would love to hear your feedback on my book and the things that you have discovered. Please connect with me – you can find me on Facebook, Messenger and Skype, or you can visit my website at http://www.thepersonalitycoach.com.au

I am available for further information about workshops, one-on-one sessions, family workshops and keynote talks via email at thepersonalitycoach@gmail.com

Or Facebook: Kate Mason The Personality Coach

I look forward to hearing from you.

Kate x

Kate Mason
The Personality Coach

RESOURCES

Books

1. *Introduction to Type* by Isabelle Briggs Myers

2. *You've got Personality* by Mary McGuiness

3. *Personality Plus* by Florence Littauer

Online resources

1. ap.themyersbriggs.com (MBTI Australia)

2. capt.org (Centre for Applications of Psychological Type, a non-profit organisation that supports research of the MBTI instrument. Founded by Isabel Myers and Mary McCaulley, PhD)

3. personalityjunkie.com

4. psychologyjunkie.com

5. keirsey.com

APPENDIX: ACTIVE LISTENING

Active listening is a process of listening that involves giving your full attention to the person being heard, whether that person is your partner, your child or a friend. Active listening means that you stop whatever you are doing and listen. Put down your smartphone, mute the TV, close the computer, put the kitchen knife down, leave the washing in the laundry basket for the moment, then either stand or sit down with the person who wants to talk to you and *listen*. I mean *really listen*.

Turn your body towards the speaker (but not so close that you invade their personal space), rest your eyes upon them (but not so intensely that you're staring at them), and only use your mouth to ask questions about the subject that they wish to talk about. No interruptions. If they are discussing a topic that you would like to add to … don't! This is not *your* story time; it is *theirs*. If they want to talk about an issue with their best friend at school, don't tell them all about *your* best friend at school. When appropriate, ask thoughtful questions about the topic at hand, such as, 'So, is Fred your best friend, or do you have others?'

Follow the trail of conversation, without giving your opinion or describing your experiences. You will find that children/partners/friends will open up to you and feel so valued that they will share 'stuff' that you might never have heard before. Keep their confidence about these conversations and you will become a wonderful listener, privy to many valuable insights about the people you care about.

And remember, you will get your turn to talk later.

This style of listening must be learned and will always be a work in progress. We do not always get it right, and even though I've been practising for years, sometimes a better story just pops out of my mouth when I should be keeping it shut. But I always give active listening my best shot, and it is worth the effort when I am rewarded with knowing the inside thoughts and ideas of my family.

Try this sometime – you will be amazed.

www.ingramcontent.com/pod-product-compliance
Lightning Source LLC
Chambersburg PA
CBHW061200070526
44579CB00009B/78